THE LEAST WORST TELEVISION IN THE WORLD

By the same author

THE LEAST WORST TELEVISION IN THE WORLD

by

Milton Shulman

BARRIE & JENKINS
LONDON

© Milton Shulman 1973
First published 1973 by
Barrie & Jenkins Ltd
24 Highbury Crescent
London N5 1RX

ISBN 0 214 66853 3

PRINTED IN GREAT BRITAIN BY
WESTERN PRINTING SERVICES LTD, BRISTOL.

CONTENTS

INTRODUCTION

When, in November 1972, the BBC celebrated its fiftieth anniversary, even the Queen and the Prime Minister joined in the cascade of congratulations that showered upon the Corporation. Judging by the beaming compliments all round, who could doubt the BBC's oft-repeated claim that it provided the best television service in the world? If there was any embarassment at the disparity between the back-slapping for the occasion and the back-stabbing that has been going on against the BBC for many years, the Establishment managed to conceal it. No one wanted to spoil the party. It could also be said that whatever one might think of the BBC in the 1970s, its past achievements amply justified its moment of unalloyed glory.

But even the more laudatory commentators could not suppress their mixed feelings about the course of broadcasting. Said the *Financial Times* on 2 November 1972: 'There is an increasing amount of evidence that suggests that too much television might in some way be harmful, either by propagating half-baked thoughts, or by encouraging violence, or by distorting everyone's vision of the world. . . . The BBC will be shirking its duty if, in its next few years, it fails to get to grips with this fundamental problem in order to see whether its output ought to be tailored, or curtailed (or possibly expanded) for the good of the society it serves.'

When T. C. Worsley, one of the most perceptive TV critics in Britain gave up his job, he wrote on October 18, 1972 in the *Financial Times*, 'Do I, looking back ten years, find things better by comparison or worse? I unhesitatingly say worse.' When Maurice Wiggin, *The Sunday Times* critic for twenty years, put down his pen on retirement, he wrote, 'I don't know where television is heading, but I do know that it seems on the whole rougher, cheaper, shoddier, dirtier, nastier and more vulgar than it need be, and than it used to be.' Every serious independent investigation of television in recent years has echoed these misgivings. The Pilkington Committee in 1960 gave a seal of approval to the BBC but was scathing about the record of the commercial channel. A Select Committee of the House of

Commons, after months of hearings, expressed extreme dissatisfaction in October 1972, with the manner in which the Independent Broadcasting Authority (formerly the ITV) had allowed the quality of commercial programmes to fall below statutory requirements. Every independent group that has studied the totality of the TV output—advertisers, trade unions, industry, the Tory Bow Group—has advocated either some fresh thinking about British television or a re-structuring of broadcasting.

How, then, does this unanimity of concern amongst those who have conscientiously investigated the medium square with the self-satisfied assertions of broadcasters and a few politicians that British television is the best in the world? It is in an attempt to trace the causes of that unease that these pages have been written. Although it describes the earliest days of the medium, this book has no pretentions towards being a history of British broadcasting. Many of the most formidable TV names and many of the most famous programmes do not appear, or get hardly a mention, in this volume. It is a personal survey of how television has developed and, in my opinion, how it has deteriorated. In such a tale of rise and decline, the compromises, the shortcomings, the scandals of the medium tend to overshadow the achievements and the successes. If they do, my book may act as some counterweight to the load of complacency and self-congratulation that is pumped out by the press officers of the BBC and the commercial companies.

More important, however, than revealing the cosmetic job that has been done on the warts of the medium, I hope to show the slipshod, arbitrary, chaotic, petulant, and casual way in which some of the major decisions affecting television have been taken. What is missing from the national planning about television is any serious or hard thinking about the power of the box and the relationship between such power and the state. It is this failure to realize that this harmless toy could develop into an uncontrollable monster that accounts for the dubious direction British television has now taken and for the anxiety it now produces in growing numbers of people.

Whether television can exert the influences being claimed for it, is only fleetingly touched upon in this volume. I have attempted to substantiate in another book, *The Ravenous Eye*, the case for believing that television is the most radical medium for change and disruption—if improperly understood and organized—that man has ever experienced. It is my hope that this account of the British television will make some contribution to a climate of opinion which will ensure that it truly deserves the accolade of being 'the best' rather than 'the least worst' in the world.

Although I worked in television for six years, it has been my eight years as a television critic for the *Evening Standard* that has given me the opportunity to survey the panorama of the medium rather than just a narrow view from the foothills. It is because I have had the unfettered luxury of being able weekly to think aloud about the structure, the trends and the goals of the medium that this book was at all possible. For allowing me without restraint to express my sometimes idiosyncratic, sometimes unrestrained, sometimes perverse, sometimes impertinent views about television and those who work in it, I must thank Sir Max Aitken, Chairman of Beaverbrook Newspapers, and Charles Wintour, editor of the *Evening Standard*. They could never have agreed with all I said—nobody could—but their reservations—when and if they had them—were never communicated to me. I should also say a grateful word to my wife, Drusilla, who for many years has patiently listened to me arguing with myself about the diverse aspects of television contained in this book.

January, 1973

CHAPTER I

THE EASY MONEY SCANDAL

No one denies that the profits made out of commercial television were a national scandal which should have undermined the position of the Macmillan Government more seriously than the Profumo affair. What is beyond comprehension is that the same procedure should have been allowed to repeat itself under a Labour Government without a murmur.—'C,' a prominent statesman, in *The Times*, 10 June 1968.

The deterioration of BBC standards began with the drive to compete for viewing figures with commercial television. . . . A truly paternalistic government would put matters right once and for all by undoing the harm done to this invaluable medium of entertainment and education in the Television Act of 1954.—Bernard Hollowood, Editor of *Punch*, 30 October 1968.

Television has become so pervasive and permanent an aspect of the cultural life of countries like Britain, America, Canada, and Australia that it is always surprising to realize how young and novel a medium it really is. Before World War II Britain was the only country transmitting regular television programmes. They began in 1936, and by the outbreak of war there were only about 20,000 receivers in the entire country. From 1939 to 1947 there was no television service because of the war. Even as late as 1947 only three countries in the world—Britain, America, and Russia—provided regular television broadcasting. France did not start until 1949.[1]

Yet in the short space of two decades—a flick of history's eyelid—television has raced into the consciousness of most of mankind. Over one hundred and ten countries now have a television service. In both the United Kingdom and the United States over 95 % of all families have a television set. This means that in Britain about 18,500,000 homes possess television sets. There are twice as many television sets as there are motor cars or refrigerators. There are more television sets to be stared at than bath-tubs to be washed in. It is estimated that *every night* twenty million viewers in Britain are gazing at the small screen. Each person views between two and a half and three hours per day. It is interesting to compare the speed of this development with the speed of the spread of the printing press—the technological revolution to which television is most often compared. How many printed books were being read

twenty-five years after Gutenberg had demonstrated the
wonders of moveable type! 'In 1500,' writes Marshall McLuhan,
'nobody knew how to market or distribute the mass-produced
book.'[2]

It may be that the haste with which this electronic web has
fastened itself upon industrialized Western societies accounts in
some measure for the slipshod, casual, almost anarchic, nature
of its development. The public wanted television; the politicians
were ready to give the public what it wanted as quickly as
possible. Aside from some provisions for the safeguarding of
political balance, Governments were not over-concerned with
the content or organization of a medium which they mentally
dismissed as something with as much cultural significance as
home movies. Only the most cursory thought was given to its
philosophical, moral, and social implications. No thought at all
was given to the possibility that television might drastically
change people's attitudes or that the very speed of the change
might create certain stresses and pressures for which society
would be unprepared.

Although in Britain two committees—the Beveridge Committee in 1950 and the Pilkington Committee in 1960—provided thoughtful reports on the state of broadcasting in this
country, their main recommendations—Beveridge wanted the
continuation of the BBC monopoly and Pilkington wanted a
thorough restructuring of commercial television—were over-
ruled with almost cavalier contempt by the Governments
concerned.

In both Britain and America it was the approach and spirit
of radio broadcasting that largely determined the cultural and
economic guide-lines upon which television was modelled in
its early days. Radio had played a relatively respectable,
stabilizing, and reassuring part in the life of English-speaking
countries during the 1920s and 1930s. Television, it was
reasoned, should do much the same. Unsettling ideas about
the differences in impact of aural and visual stimuli, in the
degree of involvement demanded by television as compared to
radio and, consequently, in the number of hours that should be
allowed for each medium, seemed to worry only the academics.

Thus in America, television—like radio—became a medium
financed by advertisers and primarily devoted to the demands
of the market-place. In the satisfactory fulfilment of that function, it catered to the masses, deified the ratings, paid lip-
service to public affairs, neglected the minorities. The Federal
Communications Commission, set up to supervise the licensing

of American stations, has had little influence in diverting television from its major, all-absorbing goal of providing entertainment in the interest of profits.

The dominating influence on the character of British broadcasting was the personality of Lord Reith, the formidable Scotsman, Director General of the BBC from 1927 to 1938, who died in 1971 at the age of seventy-two. It was Reith's efforts that ushered in the British Broadcasting Corporation in 1927 under a Royal Charter rather than a Parliamentary statute. The commercial channel, on the other hand, was instituted by statute in 1954. The BBC's status as a public corporation gave it an unexpected amount of freedom from Government control, and although in practice it has been brought into line with the statutory restrictions that govern the ITV, it still enjoys, at least on paper, a degree of independence denied its rival channel.

But even more important than this charter of independence was the philosophy of dedicated public service that Reith brought to the BBC. Armed with an uncompromising belief in Christian duty, he insisted that programmes should never fall below the ethical and intellectual standards which he felt to be in the public interest. His was an unashamedly paternalistic regime, in which there was no place for such irresponsible notions as giving the public what it wanted. The public would get what Reith and his colleagues thought was good for them and the nation.

'We have done our best to found a tradition of public service rather than public exploitation,' he wrote in 1931. 'The broadcasting system of a nation is a mirror of that nation's conscience. . . . This is the trust which we have assumed and we did not assume it lightly. There are no loopholes to duty, and no compromise is possible with what one considers to be right. The generation of tomorrow will judge us not just in terms of the amusement we have given, but by what we have stood for in the past and may still stand for in the future. If the day should come—and I don't think it will—when broadcasting should play to the lowest rather than the highest in man, then will the country itself have fallen very low.'[3]

Under Reith the Establishment had few things to fear from radio broadcasting. His policy encouraged respect for national institutions, support of the social system, the upholding of the Church as the main arbiter of moral and ethical problems, and a neutralization of social and political controversy. Sunday broadcasting, devoted to faith and solemnity, consisted mainly of Church services, symphony concerts, and serious talk. Such frivolities as jazz or variety programmes, Reith asserted, would never be heard on Sundays.

BBC announcers, punctiliously garbed in dinner jackets, spoke an impeccable English which was impersonal, non-working class, and non-regional. It was the voice of the responsible, the respectable, and the genteel elements in British society. It was not until 1928 that the ban on controversy was lifted and political discussion became possible. The fourteen-day rule, which insisted that a fortnight's gap had to intervene between anything that came up in Parliament and any comment about it on radio and television, was not abandoned until 1956. Satirical shows mocking public figures and unscripted, argumentative current affairs programmes—so much a part of broadcasting in the 1960s—were unthinkable in Reith's era of the 1930s.

'He was no mere impressario, nor a purveyor of news alone, but the proprietor of a great missionary enterprise and the chief executive of an as yet unborn Arts Council,' wrote Denis Forman, a Managing Director of Granada TV. 'Those selected for duty naturally reflected something of his idealism and tended to agree with his principles. They were an oligarchy of rare individuals, with one foot in Bloomsbury and one in All Souls; and all were imbued with a proselytizing zeal for the best in English middle-class culture.

'Such a regime implied that if some things were "good" and should be broadcast, others were "bad" and should not. If one scans the pages of the *Radio Times* and *TV Times* and strikes out those programmes which Reith would not have permitted, it is likely that between one-quarter and one-third of what is at present on the air would disappear.'[4]

In addition to principles and ideals, Reith gave the BBC a backbone. As a public corporation established by Royal Charter, the limitations on its independence were far fewer than had been set up by statute. True, the Postmaster General, now called the Minister of Posts and Telecommunications, determines the number of hours of permitted broadcasting and the size of the licence fee, and he theoretically has the right to forbid the broadcast of any programme, yet in the BBC's entire history no particular programme has been officially vetoed. Nor is there any other Minister in the House of Commons responsible for BBC broadcasts. MPs who ask indignant questions in the House about the suitability or desirability of certain programmes like *Till Death Us Do Part* or *That Was The Week*

That Was are venting their spleen in a constitutional vacuum. There is nobody in a position to reply.

This means that to get the BBC to do what it wants, a Government or Prime Minister must resort to more discreet and devious methods than the blunt exercise of direct power. Reith demonstrated that even in a moment of national crisis the BBC would not bow to the dictates of politicians. During the General Strike of 1926, Churchill at the Home Office wanted to take over the BBC and use it as an instrument of Government propaganda. Reith argued that the BBC should be allowed to put out an independent news service giving an impartial account of the industrial struggle. Prime Minister Baldwin sided with Reith, and a precedent of independence was then established which has not been lightly questioned since.

'It was not a time for dope, even if people could have been doped,' wrote Reith afterwards. 'If we had suppressed news of any unfortunate situation arising, it might only have led to the panic of ignorance.'[5]

Thirty years later, in another moment of national crisis, the BBC responded similarly to the threat of Government control. The crisis was Suez and this time both radio and television were involved. Eden tried to get the BBC to accept the view that the invasion of Egypt in November 1956 was equivalent to a declaration of war and that under such circumstances the Government had the right to take over the broadcasting apparatus and use it as it saw fit. This time the will of the Government was determinedly opposed by Sir Norman Bottomley, Acting Director General in Sir Ian Jacob's absence, and by his Chief Assistant, Harman Grisewood.

Grisewood had been told that 'the Prime Minister had instructed the Lord Chancellor (Lord Kilmuir) to prepare an instrument which would take over the BBC altogether and subject it wholly to the will of the Government.' The matter reached the BBC's Board of Governors on a supplementary issue. Should the BBC overseas bulletins, which would be heard by the troops waiting to invade Egypt, be allowed to contain extracts of the arguments being used by Opposition leaders like Gaitskell and newspapers like the *Manchester Guardian* who were vehemently attacking the Government's actions? The Board firmly backed the view that the BBC's policy of impartial reporting had to be maintained. Faced with this firm front, Eden did not push his plans any further.

'It was the BBC's duty to report to the people any opinions

about the question which were important enough to affect the outcome,' wrote Grisewood in his autobiography, *One Thing at a Time*. 'This was bed-rock democracy. The people of the country had a right to know as much about the issue as fair reporting could supply; and a right, of course, to hear the arguments of Government and Opposition. In spite of the PM, Suez was a parliamentary issue. It was not a national war; the BBC should not and would not be manoeuvred into acting as though it were.'[6]

When one compares this affirmation of principle with the arguments Reith used for news impartiality during the General Strike, it is amazing how alike in tone and spirit they are. Although about half-a-dozen Directors General had sat in Reith's chair in the years between his departure and Suez, the tradition of independence from Government dictate had already grown deep and stubborn roots. Any politician in the future who tried to tug out these roots too violently might find himself flat on his back in the midst of a constitutional crisis and surrounded by an outraged public.

The policy of independence from Government interference was further entrenched in the political conscience of the nation when Grisewood's revelations about Suez were raised in the Commons on 6 May 1968. Replying to a Member's question about the possibility of a weaker, less principled and more corruptible body of governors and staff at the BBC one day, yielding to threats and pressures from some future Prime Minister, Roy Mason, the Labour Postmaster General, gave an almost unequivocal guarantee of freedom to the broadcasting authorities:

'Once any government decides to control in some measure, the programme content of a broadcasting service,' said Mr Mason, 'it sets off on a steep and slippery slope. The BBC and ITA are independent. How then, twelve years after are we to regard this episode, or Mr Grisewood's account of it? Surely as an aberration. Since the earliest days of broadcasting the independence of the BBC has been regarded as a fundamental principle. This principle has been reaffirmed many times. . . . The check to a threat by any government to the independence of the broadcasting authorities lay in the willingness of the governors to face that threat. The ultimate check was that of opinion, and particularly of Parliamentary opinion.'

But it would be naïve to assume that this ringing defence of broadcasting freedom means that the BBC and the ITA are at liberty to run their channels exactly as they wish. Politicians fear the power of the medium far too much for that. Under the guise of that ambiguous word 'balance'—which represents an agreed observance of political neutrality by the broadcasting authorities—the political parties are zealously on the alert for any programme, gesture, or word on television that might seem to give unfair advantage to one of the other sides. It is this niggling surveillance, this constant bickering about rudeness by interviewers or unfair treatment, that constitutes the real threat to the independence of television. As we shall see in these pages, Governments have got concessions from broadcasting authorities by more subtle means than the wielding of big sticks.

It was a philosophy of public service and a determination to be independent that television in Britain inherited from radio. In the years immediately following World War II the stern idealism of Lord Reith still hovered over the BBC like a nagging conscience. In those years, too, television was very much the junior brother of radio—watched suspiciously and somewhat enviously by its more respectable partner and firmly kept in its place. As late as 1953, the *Radio Times*—the official programme magazine of the Corporation—devoted the front and major share of its pages to the personalities and activities of the microphone. The programmes of the small screen were cramped in a miserly four pages at the tail-end of the publication.

It was clear, however, that the BBC's domination of the broadcasting media could not go on unchallenged forever. As early as 1948 forces were being mobilized for an assault on the BBC's monopoly position. The end of the war not only brought in a Labour Government but it ushered in a sceptical mood and a questioning of old values and institutions. If the Empire could be changed, what was so inviolate about the BBC? The old paternalism no longer suited the times. There was an aura of ossification about the Corporation—smug in its reputation, conformist in its attitudes, deferential to the powers-that-be, unadventurous in its handling of television. Above all, 'monopoly' had become an extremely dirty word.

For a moment it looked as if the reformers would be checked. The Beveridge Committee concluded—with only Selwyn Lloyd, MP dissenting—that the BBC's monopoly should be maintained. But before their recommendations could be implemented, the Labour Government had been defeated in the election of 1951 and the Tories felt they had the right to re-think the whole matter once again.

It cannot be said that there was any great public clamour for a television service financed by advertising. But opinion polls

conducted at the time indicated that the British did want a
second service. If the BBC had given it to them they would
have been content. They would have reacted strongly only if
their licence fees had been unduly raised to finance such a
service. On the other hand, if more television were provided
by some other financial device or by some other body, they
were prepared to accept the solution with equanimity. The
prospect of the BBC losing its monopoly roused no passion in
the streets. As an issue it stimulated little more than apathy
among the people.

The battle for the future and the soul of television was therefore fought out between two opposing pressure groups. The
protagonists could not easily be split according to party lines.
While the vast bulk of the Labour Party were against television
dominated by financial interests, the Tories were furiously
divided. Conservatives like Lord Hailsham thought that commercial television could only mean a sell-out of moral values;
conservatives like Lord Woolton actively supported those out
to break the Corporation's monopoly.

It was, however, a sustained campaign of propaganda and
persuasion conducted by a small group of Tory MPs and
businessmen that eventually won the day. If one had to chose
a single individual who might be said to have brought commercial television into being it would be Norman Collins. A
former Controller of BBC TV, Collins left the BBC in 1950,
after he was denied a promotion to Director of BBC TV, and
campaigned vigorously for four years to bring about the end
of the Corporation's monopoly.

'It is no reflection on the personal integrity of these individuals and others who were to join them, and no disparagement
of their devotion to antimonopoly, freedom of choice, and
competition, to note that the pioneers and most of their active
colleagues were fortunate that their political principles coincided
with their career and financial interest,'[7] wrote H. H. Wilson
in *Pressure Group*, an excellent and detailed account of the way
in which commercial television came into being.

There was one man in those early, lobbying days who could
have decisively stifled the birth of commercial television. That
was the Conservative Prime Minister, Sir Winston Churchill.
Churchill was mildly contemptuous of the idea of commercial
television, which he referred to as a 'tuppenny Punch and Judy
show.'[8] His personal experiences with the BBC before the war,
however, had not unduly endeared him to the Corporation.
There had been his differences with Reith over the use of the

BBC during the General Strike. There was also some brooding resentment against the BBC because it had not in the thirties given him access to the microphone to broadcast his pungent and controversial views on Indian policy and rearmament. He stood on the side-lines neither encouraging nor discouraging the forces busily undermining the BBC's domination of broadcasting. Eventually he came out against the BBC. '... The longer I have studied this matter and watched the development in the last few months, the more I am convinced that the present monopoly should not continue,' he said.[9]

In May 1952, the Conservative Government issued a White Paper which sounded the death knell of the BBC monopoly. Although it acknowledged the principle that the BBC alone would receive the revenue from broadcasting-receiving licences, it also concluded that 'in the expanding field of television, provision should be made to permit some element of competition.' Belatedly, the defenders of the BBC sprung to action.

In the debate in the House of Lords, Reith himself thundered a hyperbolic denunciation of the Government's plans. 'Somebody introduced Christianity into England,' he said, 'and somebody introduced smallpox, bubonic plague and the Black Death. Somebody is minded now to introduce sponsored broadcasting. ... Need we be ashamed of moral values, or of intellectual and ethical objectives? It is these that are here and now at stake.'

The Labour Opposition, having missed their chance of doing something constructive about television when they were in power, now donned a mantle of outraged indignation. In the debate on the White Paper in the Commons Patrick Gordon Walker, an Opposition spokesman, turned the affair into a party issue by declaring, 'We shall certainly not carry on the policy implied in this non-exclusive licence ... we reserve our full right to frustrate this retrograde innovation.'[10]

Thoroughly alarmed at the prospect of deteriorating television standards, the defenders of the BBC now roused themselves into a determined effort to get the Government to reverse its decision. They formed an anti-commercial television lobby called the National Television Council, bristling with bishops, university vice-chancellors, and formidable figures like Lady Violet Bonham Carter, Lord Hailsham, Lord Waverley, Lord Halifax, Lord Simon of Wythenshawe, and Christopher Mayhew, MP.

But too late: the issue was now drawn along party lines. When that happens, altruism, logic, and the national good are likely to be the victims. There followed two years of argument, lobbying, leader columns, letters to editors, which hardened rather than shifted party positions. On 15 June 1953, Labour's leader, Clement Attlee, pledged a reversal of the Tory plunge into commercial television.

'If the Conservative Party allowed television to pass into the hands of private profiteers,' he told the Commons, 'Labour would have to alter the situation when it returned to power.'

The threat merely strengthened Tory determination to push the Bill through. When the vote was finally taken on 4 March 1954, MPs were not allowed the moral luxury of a free vote. The Whips were firmly on. Every Tory toed the line. The Bill was passed by 296 to 269. The Television Act became law on 30 July 1954.

'Britain was given commercial television against the advice of all the nominal leaders of society in education, religion and culture,' wrote Professor Wilson, 'as well as significant sections of the business community. At no time was the British electorate, or even the rank and file Conservative voter, given an opportunity of passing on the merits of the case.'[11]

The opponents of the Bill, however, had managed to drag one important concession from the Government. There was to be no sponsored television in Britain. Advertisers would not be able to prepare, subsidize, or control their own programmes. The programme content was entirely the responsibility of the companies that were to be given franchises. Programmes were to be kept rigidly independent of the influence and pressures of advertisers. Thus it was hoped that the worst aspect of the American system—where television had become little more than an adjunct of the market-place—would be avoided in Britain.

While this decision appeased some of the anti-commercial faction, it cast prospective candidates for the new stations into a deep gloom. After all, the main object of all the campaigning and the lobbying was to make money for advertisers, advertising agents, and owners of the commercial franchises. To quote Professor Wilson again, 'Throughout the controversy it was apparent that the commercial advocates were contemptuous of efforts to uphold either cultural or intellectual standards; the decisive consideration was that television was a great marketing device.'[12]

Was there money to be made if advertisers could not sponsor their own programmes? The experience of the American networks indicated that it was not possible. To many potential applicants for television licences, it looked as if they were being offered merely an opportunity to lose millions. When the Independent Television Authority, set up to administer the Act under the chairmanship of art historian Sir Kenneth Clark, advertised for applications for the new stations, only twenty-five groups applied.

The ITA, relying on a policy of regional devolution, had divided the country into twelve regions—London, the Midlands, and the North because of their size were divided between two companies. Thus fourteen companies were granted franchises and took up their responsibilities as soon as transmitter and other facilities were ready.

The first company to go on the air on 22 September 1955 was Associated Rediffusion, responsible for Monday-to-Friday programmes in the London area. In its first two years it lost £2,880,349. So devastating were these losses—and so gloomy was the profit forecast—that Associated Newspapers (owners of the *Daily Mail, Sketch,* and other publications) decided to sell their substantial share in the company. Associated Television (ATV), which went on the air at the same time and was to provide weekend programmes for London as well as weekday programmes in the Midlands, lost £602,715 in the first seven months of its operation. The early history of most of the other companies showed similar financial failure.

When the tide turned, however, the commercial companies were overwhelmed by an avalanche of money. In the year 1958 Associated Rediffusion made a net profit of £4,889,015, which adequately compensated them for their previous losses. In 1959 their net profit was over £7,000,000 and in 1960 it was almost £8,000,000. ATV's profit was over £5,000,000 annually in the years from 1959 to 1963. Granada TV, which started transmission a little later than the first companies, soon demonstrated that profits of this order were as available in the North of England as in the lush pastures of the South. The smaller regional companies also revelled in this downpour of gold. Lord Thomson, whose profits from Scottish TV helped him considerably to finance his acquisition of such important English newspapers as *The Sunday Times* and *The Times,* wrote the disarming epitaph for this period of extravagant easy money when he said that a commercial television franchise was 'a licence to print money.'[13]

It was a costly comment since it alerted public opinion to the dimensions of the scandalous profits that were being made on the basis of a Government monopoly. Not since the days of the East India Company were fortunes being made so easily. Norman Collins, one of the early protagonists for breaking through the BBC monopoly, and subsequently an executive with ATV, saw his shareholding of £2,250 expand in a few years to something like £500,000.

Millionaires in television were being created at an almost indecent rate. Collins himself had the grace in 1961 to describe the profits being made as 'colossal' and 'immoral.'

Now what sort of service were the new companies providing in return for such riches? From the beginning they concentrated on popular appeal, and, backed by a benevolent ITA, aimed relentlessly at the lowest common level of public taste. With an occasional obeisance in the direction of drama or documentaries—perhaps one or two hours a week at peak time—the companies were determined to make their channel primarily a transmitter of entertainment. In the prime hours— between 7 and 10 pm when viewing was at its highest— variety, quiz games, westerns, thriller series, old films, and soap opera were shown 90% of the time. Only in the field of news—where the Independent Television News (ITN), backed financially by all the companies, was responsible for news bulletins—did anything fresh and really mature emerge. A less sacrosanct approach to news stories, a less obsequious manner towards politicians, and a rejection of the Reithian middle-class accent gave a brash, relaxed, enquiring atmosphere, new to this form of television journalism. In time, ITN's approach forced the BBC to abandon its previous stiffness and forelock-tugging deference to senior politicians and members of the Establishment.

As for the rest—with the exception of some regular programmes like *This Week*, *Armchair Theatre*, *What The Papers Say*—frivolity and triviality were the order of the day. The commercial channel was the place where couples in boiler suits could win refrigerators if they smashed enough balloons with needles pinned to their noses. It was the channel where silly quiz games like *Double Your Money* and *Take Your Pick* (in which you might win a bedroom suite if you happened to know that Shakespeare wrote Hamlet) were kept running regularly for twelve years. It was the mausoleum for old films that the cinema had discarded. It was the haven for unimaginative westerns, fatuous adventure thrillers like *Crane* and *Riviera Police*, moronic panel shows like *The Celebrity Game*. It was a stubborn bastion against any adventurous ideas.

Thus in 1962 the Pilkington Committee—set up two years

before to review the state of broadcasting in Britain and make recommendations about its future—had this to say about the performance of the commercial companies after four years:

'The causes of disquiet about, and dissatisfaction with, television are justly attributed very largely to the service of independent television; this despite the popularity of the service and the fact that many of its programmes command the largest audiences. This kind of success is not the only, and is by no means the most important, test of a good broadcasting service. It is one which can be obtained by abandoning the purposes of broadcasting.'[14]

In spite of the strictures of the Pilkington Committee the quality of the programmes on the commercial channel underwent no fundamental change. Two years after Pilkington—at the time of the General Election of 1964—the nation was still staring at—and preferring—this visual mosaic of bland, innocuous, violent, and frivolous trivia. The press at this time reflected the general disenchantment with the standard of programming that had become routine on commercial television. *The Times* wrote wearily about 'an endless belt of triviality.' *The Sun*, a left-wing newspaper, declared in a leader that too many viewers were 'insulted by the early evening procession of soap operas, imported comedies and quizzes.'

The Government, of course, in its oft-proclaimed stance of non-interference with the content of programmes on both the BBC and ITV, displayed no overt concern about this decline in standards. Nor was the ITA, under the chairmanship of Sir Ivone Kirkpatrick, who had taken over from Sir Kenneth Clark in 1957, unduly perturbed about the performance of its well-heeled wards.

'A professional diplomat, Kirkpatrick, though a man of great sensitivity,' wrote E. G. Wedell, 'had little patience with attempts to define the task of broadcasting in the light of its social significance. He thought it an over-simplification to regard television as a main factor in shaping the attitudes of society. So he did not think that it could be made to help, by means of prescription, to promote the betterment of society. Thus he had little feeling for the significance of the service in terms other than those of supply and demand.'[15]

But if no one was prepared to face a precise or constructive view about the philosophical basis of broadcasting, even the Conservative Government had to recognize that the financial scandal of vast profits out of a monopoly situation which it had created, could no longer be tolerated. The Tory Postmaster

General, Reginald Bevins, in the face of considerable opposition from commercial television interests, introduced a direct tax—over and above their normal taxes—which considerably reduced the flow of easy money into their swollen coffers. From 1964 to 1969 the companies paid a levy on their net advertising revenue on the basis of a graduated scale. They paid nothing on the first £1,500,000 of advertising revenue, 25% on the next £6,000,000, and all of 85% on anything over £7,500,000.

Inevitably there were heart-rending cries of pain and distress from the commercial companies when these terms for keeping a franchise were announced. 'To hold shares in some of the ITV companies,' said Norman Collins at the time, 'is to be the possessor, if I may adapt a famous phrase, of a licence to lose money.'

Mr Collins need never have worried. The torrent of money had merely been curbed to a generous flow. From 1964 to 1969, in spite of the levy, the major companies had little difficulty in achieving *net* profits of around £1,500,000 and more annually. Since this was a return of about 25% on capital invested and came from a non-risk, competition-free business, it cannot be said that the Government was setting out to turn its newly created millionaires into paupers. No wonder that when the Labour Government called for applications for new franchises in 1968, there was an almost indecent stampede of financiers, businesses, merchant banks, show business personalities, peers of the realm, and newspaper proprietors eager to get some share of this money-on-a-plate. Their accountants and their slide-rules—making astute calculations—assured them that levy or not, there were still good pickings to be dug from the commercial television gold mine. But, as we shall see, another Government twist of the economic screw in the Roy Jenkins Budget of 1969, together with the increased cost of introducing colour television, seriously confounded some of these happy prognostications.

It should also be noted that the men who owned and controlled these independent companies had not been chosen because they had demonstrated any special aptitude or will to educate, uplift, or inform the public, or because they had any experience in the administration or organization of television broadcasting. They were nearly all amateurs, selected by the ITA because they were either financially responsible or had some experience in the areas of show-business or newspapers.

The main shareholders of Associated TV included showmen Lew Grade, Val Parnell, and Prince Littler, the stockbroker

Lord Renwick, the electrical company Pye, and the *Daily Mirror*.

The weekday London company, Associated Rediffusion, was owned by a group of City businessmen with very limited experience in any branch of the entertainment or newspaper business. Board members like the accountant John Spencer Wills and the radio engineer Paul Adorian—who represented British Electric Traction and Rediffusion, a piped-radio company— made almost a fetish of not becoming involved in the programme content of the company. As their General Manager, they appointed an ex-naval officer, Captain Tom Brownrigg, who was always pleased to tell one that when he first went to Hollywood to buy programmes for the company he was introduced to stars like Bing Crosby and Bob Hope and hadn't the faintest idea of who they were or what they did.

Granada TV, the company with the Northern franchise, was owned primarily by the Bernstein family, with the energetic, autocratic, patrician Sidney, now Lord Bernstein, as its Chairman. The family had made its money from cinemas, and backed by a substantial loan from one of the major banks, it was able to finance Granada single-handed. Granada was the only major television company that could be said to be dominated by a single individual. Because Bernstein was a life-long Socialist, Granada provided the necessary political balance in the distribution of these contracts. But Sidney Bernstein's Socialism, his interest in modern art, and his passion for intellectual discussion and argument never dulled his enthusiasm for show business or his appreciation of the financial potential of his company. In every Granada office there hung a framed lithograph of the famous American showman Phineas T. Barnum to remind his young, sometimes idealistic, employees that even the most serious and controversial programmes could best be sold to the public in bright, even razzle-dazzle, presentation packets. Barnum's favourite dictum 'there's a sucker born every minute' guided the behaviour of the Granada workers even in their most idealistic ventures.

The other major company, ABC Television, was smaller than Rediffusion, ATV, and Granada since it was responsible only for weekend programmes in the North and the Midlands. It, too, was primarily attuned to the demands of show business. It was owned and controlled by Associated British Picture Corporation, of which a major shareholder, when it received its franchise, was Warner Brothers, the American film company. Before they came into television, this company's chief activity was running the second largest cinema chain in Britain—about four hundred cinemas. It also had a small reputation as a film producer.

The ten other companies* were much smaller than the Big Four, and from a production standpoint their efforts at original programming were largely confined to small, inexpensive studio shows with a regional flavour. Occasionally they offered a play or a documentary to the whole network, but for the most part they were squeezed out of any serious creative television work by the large four companies. Since making programmes entailed an unnecessary expense, it cannot be said that many of the regional companies protested over-vigorously at their exclusion from the national network. All of these companies, too, made a great deal of money.

Thus it can be seen that the men to whom the Independent Television Authority handed over the destiny of the commercial channel were very much the same breed. The men with a background of the cinema, variety, or the theatre thought of the small box merely as a midget Odeon, Granada, or Palladium. They brought to their new jobs the concepts and attitudes which guided them when they made their livings entertaining the masses. They realized that a certain lip-service had to be paid to the informative and educational functions of the medium. But the few plays, current affairs shows, and documentaries were never more than a thin cultural dressing, ostentatiously displayed in their annual reports and in advertisements in the more serious newspapers or weeklies.

In 1964, when the Labour Party came to power, it could be said the most dire prognostications of those of its spokesmen who had opposed the introduction of the second channel had been more or less justified. The independent enquiry of the Pilkington Committee had found that the level of programmes on the commercial channel had seriously lowered the prevailing standards of British television. The triteness, the sameness, the cheapness of the bulk of the commercial output had been constantly attacked by critics and editors in the press, but they had made little impact on those who ran the companies.

The country had witnessed a major financial scandal in which, through a Government monopoly, a few men had

* Scottish TV (for Central Scotland), Anglia (for the East of England), Border (for the Borders), Tyne Tees (for North-East England), Grampian (for North-East Scotland), Southern (for the South), Westward (for South-West England), TWW (for Wales and the West), Ulster (for Northern Ireland), and Channel (for Channel Islands).

received returns on their investments out of all proportion to either the capital they had risked or the contributions they were making to the nation. A Socialist Government would presumably have been shocked and sickened by the spectacle.

Even worse, a large share of this money was siphoned out of television never to return to it. Conscious of the ephemeral nature of their franchises—their first contracts ran for ten years—the companies diversified as much money as they could into other enterprises which would guarantee shareholders continuing dividends in the event that their contracts were not renewed. They bought sports stadiums, television-rental shops, property companies, optical firms, publishing houses, sweet shops, hotels, agencies, and a host of other businesses. It has been estimated that over £80,000,000 was diversified in this way in the first ten years of commercial television. And once it was gone, it was no longer available for spending on programmes or studios or experiments or capital equipment or the fees and wages of those artists and technicians working in the medium. Although a perfectly legitimate business device—some might even argue an essential duty of directors to their shareholders—this channelling of their cash into activities not remotely connected with television hardly indicated any long-term faith in either the prospects or the value of the medium.

But the philosophy of the commercial television companies had no place for serious commitment to the medium. They provided a service. It was an adequate service. Why risk money, for example, in producing programmes for export? Only one company, ATV, determinedly took on the hazardous task of trying to make programmes which might be acceptable in the American market. It cannot be said that series like *The Saint* or *Sir Francis Drake* did much to raise the standards of television entertainment, but they did eventually bring into Britain much needed foreign currency. ABC, with their series *The Avengers*, also succeeded in breaking into the lush American networks in a small way. But, on the whole, the companies were not prepared to gamble their profits in producing programmes with the technical quality or sophisticated story-line which would be needed to compete with expensive American series for the television markets of the world.

Thus when Harold Wilson became Prime Minister in 1964, commercial television had managed to live up to the worst expectations of its most severe critics. There were only two things that could be said for it. It was very popular, and it maintained a strict, almost eunuch-like neutrality on political issues. For these benefits, the nation was saddled with a broadcasting service whose standards of programming had been found seriously wanting by the Pilkington Committee and whose administration of a monopoly had been characterized by greed, self-interest, and a smug unconcern about either the expansion or the potential of the medium. Surely any Government, and particularly a Labour Government, would do something about it! Yet nothing was done.

CHAPTER II

THE POLITICIANS TAKE OVER

Independent Television has become part of our national anatomy. More than that it has become part of our social system and part of our national way of life. . . . —The Rt Hon. Harold Wilson at a Guildhall banquet celebrating ten years of Independent Television.

He's the only really competent political television performer this country has produced. . . . —Lord Poole, former Chairman of the Conservative Party, on Harold Wilson.

Politicians have always insisted, hand on heart, that the independence of British broadcasting has become an almost inviolate constitutional principle. As we have seen, in matters of crisis like the General Strike and Suez, this principle has sometimes been subjected to severe strain and buffeting. But with the determination of men like Reith and Bottomley, the BBC had managed to resist such pressures and kept the politicians firmly in their place.

Harold Wilson was the first Labour Prime Minister to have to live with television as a major determining force in the country's political affairs. When Attlee led the country in the immediate post-war years, television was an insignificant domestic toy of minimal social significance. In 1951, when Attlee's Government was defeated, less than 10% of British homes possessed a television set.

But in the 1960s television as a potential conditioning medium was far more significant. By 1964 there were television sets in the homes of more than 90% of the electorate. Politicians were discovering that you could no longer treat the television studio as casually as a town hall. There were unfamiliar factors like make-up, personal mannerisms, lighting that might incur unpredictable responses from television audiences. Harold Wilson had carefully read Theodore White's book *The Making of the President*, which describes in detail the famous Nixon-Kennedy television debates. Was it the bad lighting which gave him the heavy beard of 'a bad guy' that had taken significant marginal votes from Nixon? Was Nixon wise in giving such a public platform to an opponent who was far less known than himself? Was it the arguments or the image that swayed most voters in these confrontations? The use of television had suddenly become more important than the traditional means of gaining support—door-to-door canvassing or full and favourable reportage in the newspapers.

With the British press 80% or more openly anti-Labour, it was always understandable that any Labour leader would be sensitive to the manner in which television reported, scrutinized, and analysed political affairs. The rules about balance which had been written into the Television Act were tenaciously relied upon by Labour's press officers at Transport House. But accusations of unfair distribution of programme minutes were common to both parties.

With his acute political antennae, Harold Wilson was almost inordinately conscious of the press and television as media that had to be understood and manipulated by any politician seeking supreme power in Britain. From the moment he was elected leader of the Labour Party on 14 February 1963, having defeated George Brown by 144 votes to 103, Wilson set out to court, shape, and bend the press and television so that, if they were not positively helpful to his interests, they would at least not damage them. He had little success with the press, but he did succeed with television. There is little doubt that the character and philosophy of British broadcasting as it enters the '70s has been moulded in no small measure by the will and activities of Harold Wilson.

Although the newspapers from time to time report quarrels between politicians and television authorities about what should or should not have gone on the air, there is a reluctance on the part of the outsider to believe that senior statesmen ever get themselves intimately involved with the minutiae of programme details. Since it illustrates, very early in his career as leader of the Labour Party, Wilson's obsession with his television image, as well as the manner in which politicians can make their demands felt by television executives, I intend to describe in some detail the circumstances surrounding a programme I produced in which Harold Wilson was the central figure.

At the time of Wilson's election as leader of the Labour Party, I was the producer at Rediffusion Television of a half-hour, fortnightly political programme called *Decision*. It was transmitted on Tuesdays, usually at the off-peak hour of 10.45 pm. Like the BBC's *Gallery*, which was its theoretical counterpart, it dealt with topical political issues and controversies. There was little difficulty in getting most of the country's leading political figures to appear on it.

A few weeks before the Parliamentary Labour Party election that would determine whether Harold Wilson or George Brown would lead the party, I had discussed with my political adviser, David Butler, an Oxford don and Britain's leading psephologist, the idea of filming a number of people—opponents and supporters of the man chosen—and asking them how they evaluated the new Labour leader and his chances of success. The plan was *not* to transmit these interviews immediately but to keep them in storage for a few months. We would then go back to these same individuals and find out from them if their opinions of the man had changed after watching him in the job for that period of time.

Thus on the very day Wilson was elected, 14 February 1963, and the following day, seven prominent figures came to Rediffusion's studios to be filmed and interviewed about the man who had just been chosen to succeed Hugh Gaitskell as Labour's leader. Ever conscious of the question of political balance, we intended the interviewees to represent a fair selection of informed political opinion. Since they had been invited to appear on the programme before the Labour Parliamentary Party election, they would have been the same speakers whether George Brown or Harold Wilson had won the leadership.

There were four politicians—the Labour MPs George Wigg and Charles Pannell, Conservative MP Ted Leather, Liberal MP Jeremy Thorpe—and three journalists—Peregrine Worsthorne, Bernard Levin, and Henry Fairlie. On an objective assessment, it could be said that this selection was weighted against Wilson because the three journalists were anti-Socialist and hardly Wilson fans. But since it was always my intention to get Harold Wilson himself on the programme and to devote at least one-third of the programme time to an interview with him, I had to restrict the number of pro-Labour participants I could include. Otherwise I would be sure to get a complaint from the Conservative Central Office arguing that this was purely a public relations job for Harold Wilson and demanding we do something similar for their party.

All seven interviewees were asked the same three questions. Do you think Harold Wilson as Labour leader will be a good thing for the party? Do you think Harold Wilson will be a good thing for the nation? What are Mr Wilson's strengths and weaknesses as a political leader? Five months later the same people were interviewed again and asked, in the light of Mr Wilson's performance, whether or not their opinions of him had changed. The programme was scheduled for transmission on 16 July 1963.

The over-all impact of these seven statements was, in my opinion, very favourable to Wilson. Four of the speakers were most flattering about Wilson's performance as party leader; three were critical. Of the four speakers who praised him, Fairlie and Jeremy Thorpe were normally anti-Labour and therefore their support might reasonably have been deemed even more significant than approval from recognized Labour men.

It was predictable that a Labour MP like Charles Pannell should say that Wilson had probably 'the best political brain today' and that in his five months' leadership 'he seems hardly to have put a foot wrong.'

It was less predictable that the right-wing journalist Henry Fairlie should offer this eulogy: 'I think it's one of the most skilful performances by any politician, certainly in my time and possibly in this century. . . . He's conveyed to the country for the first time for about ten years that the Labour Party stands for something. The fact that I don't think it does is irrelevant. I'm reporting facts.'

Bernard Levin, whose trenchant and mocking style had infuriated politicians of all persuasions when he wrote as Taper for *The Spectator*, took up an anti-Wilson position. In his first interview he said, 'In the very short run, Harold Wilson's effect on the Labour Party will be good. I think he has a superficial plausibility, brightness, quickness, agility, and certainly cleverness which will translate into dynamism that the Labour Party needs and will do it good. But I don't think it will last. . . .'

Five months later he said, 'I said basically two things about Mr Wilson. First, that his short-term effect on the Labour Party's fortunes would be very good for it, which has certainly proved the case; second, that his long-term effect, both on the party and on the country, particularly if he becomes Prime Minister, would be bad and possibly disastrous. I think that will be true and I think that I have already seen some evidence that it will be true.'

Arrangements had already been made for Harold Wilson to appear on the programme in an interview with Kenneth Harris lasting about nine minutes. Following this interview, I had also invited the Labour MP Barbara Castle and the Tory MP Charles Curran to conclude the programme with a short discussion about Wilson's impact as Labour leader in the Commons.

It was with no misgivings at all that I sent the transcript of the seven interviews to Transport House a few weeks before the date of transmission.

The first complaint that arrived from Transport House was about Bernard Levin. A press official told me in no uncertain terms that Wilson had no intention of appearing on any programme on which Levin was a participant. It is true that Levin had hardly endeared himself to the Labour leader by his campaign of constant denigration of Wilson or by his frequent reference to him as Marshal Big Mouth. Generally, Levin left the impression that he considered Wilson a devious, unprincipled twister. I felt, however, that the prerogative of choosing who was to be on the programme belonged to me as producer and not to Transport House.

A few days later Transport House was on the phone again. They said nothing about Levin. This time their complaint was that the programme was unbalanced because all three journalists on it were anti-Labour. I pointed out that both Fairlie and Thorpe had taken a pro-Wilson stand and that, in spite of the labels of the speakers, the bias of the whole item was in Wilson's favour. They did not agree. In order to right the balance would I invite on the programme an objective political correspondent. The man they suggested was David Wood of *The Times*. But the whole object of this section of the programme, I argued, was to use people whose views, at the time Wilson was elected leader, were to be contrasted with the views they held five months later. It was too late to fit in somebody fresh into this format. They were adamant. For the sake of peace, a statement by David Wood was filmed and included in the programme. (Wood knew nothing of Transport House's request for his appearance.)

'He's a contemporary figure,' said Wood. 'He speaks the language of the kind of people who are coming to the top in industry, in the universities, in education. This will make him an attractive leader. . . . I think he could be a most important and a most successful political party leader.'

After such a testimonial heaped on top of the others, I felt sure the programme would now proceed as planned. But I was wrong. A few days before Wilson himself was to be filmed, Transport House called again. They still thought the programme unbalanced. They thought that since all four journalists on the programme were non-Labour, it was only fair that someone from a left-wing paper should be included. Would I invite John Beavan (now Lord Ardwick) the *Daily Mirror* political correspondent, to give his views of Wilson? This time I firmly said no. I explained that in my opinion balance was now overwhelmingly in Wilson's favour, that any more praise for Wilson would be sure to provoke protests from the Conservatives, and that in a twenty-seven-minute programme there was no way of putting in another two-minute statement without someone else having to go. If Beavan were brought into the show Wilson's interview would have to be cut from nine to seven minutes. I didn't think that was advisable and I was sure that, on that point, Wilson would agree with me. The conversation was terminated on a distinctly chilly note.

Having assumed that my point had been made, I went ahead with arrangements for Wilson's interview with Kenneth Harris. A studio had been allotted and a camera crew was waiting in the Rediffusion building when I arrived at 9.30 on the morning of the scheduled interview. My secretary had a message for me. Mr Wilson was *not* coming. A telephone number had been left that I could call. It was Wilson's home number.

Since Wilson had appeared in a few other programmes that I had previously produced—before he became the Labour leader—I knew him moderately well. At least we were on those chummy, Christian-name terms which Labour leaders so instinctively adopt.

'Harold,' I said, hearing Wilson's voice on the other end of the line. 'I have a message that you are not coming to Rediffusion this morning. I am naturally sorry to hear that. What's the trouble?'

My bonhomie was quickly squelched. Wilson was in no mood for conviviality.

'You know perfectly well what the trouble is,' he said. 'My people have been in touch with you for weeks over this programme. I do not intend to discuss the matter with you except in the presence of your company's General Manager.'

I protested that there had been some differences of opinion about balance, but that I had thought the matter had been settled.

'You are entitled to put whatever you like on your programme,' said Wilson. 'But I am entitled not to come on it. Unless I can speak to your General Manager, I will not appear for the interview this morning.'

About an hour later we assembled in the office of Captain Brownrigg, Rediffusion's General Manager. There was Harold Wilson, accompanied by two officials from Transport House; Brownrigg, behind his desk at the head of the room; a senior

Rediffusion executive; and myself. Everyone except Wilson was clutching a transcript of the seven interviews.

Wilson began by voicing his objections to Bernard Levin. He pointed out that Levin had consistently run a denigrating vendetta against him in the columns of *The Spectator*; that Levin had written that if Wilson ever became Prime Minister he would emigrate. Wilson had been advised that many of Levin's remarks about him were defamatory and that, if he had chosen to, he could have successfully sued Levin for libel. He then went on to say that the programme as it stood was unbalanced because it did not contain a single pro-Labour journalist. He was unhappy about the choice of Barbara Castle to debate with Charles Curran the question of Wilson's impact on the Commons. He thought there were more appropriate Labour MPs that could have been given this task. He named two or three. (They were all centre or right-wing Labour men. Mrs Castle was firmly identified with the Labour left.) Wilson spoke for about ten minutes.

My own contribution to the discussion was that nothing but unfavourable publicity would result if Bernard Levin were removed from the programme at this stage. Too many people were already aware of the row that was going on with Transport House over this matter and it would be impossible to keep such a juicy political morsel out of the papers. Although I agreed that the journalists on the programme were non-left, it was even more favourable to Wilson to have praise from someone like Henry Fairlie or David Wood than from Labour's more traditional, predictable supporters. I was still convinced, in spite of other views that had been expressed, that the comments on Wilson were adequately balanced and that to bend them any further in Wilson's direction would only invite protests from the Conservative Central Office. I didn't mention Barbara Castle because it seemed irrelevant.

Captain Brownrigg, the brisk, garrulous ex-sailor who was Rediffusion's General Manager, now summed up. He leaned to the view that the comments were not unduly biased against Wilson but he was open to argument on that score. As far as Levin was concerned, he thought there was much merit in my contention that to exclude him from the programme might provoke some awkward publicity. Was Wilson adamant that Levin be taken out?

'Oh,' said Wilson, airily. 'I don't want Levin taken off the programme. I was just explaining why I didn't like being on the same programme with him. But I don't want him taken off.'

Nor, it seems, did Wilson want any of the other contributors removed. Nor was he even much troubled about the question of balance. What did he want then? He wanted Barbara Castle off the programme! He didn't think that a debate between her and Charles Curran would add much to the programme. What, then, should be put in their place? Oh, a discussion between two more journalists. Their names? He'd leave that to us in consultation with his press people. As for Mrs Castle, we needn't worry about the embarrassment of dropping her. He'd explain it all to Barbara.

And so the programme was transmitted on 17 July 1963 with a discussion between the political correspondents of *The Observer* and *The Sunday Times* taking the place of the Castle-Curran discussion. Everything else remained exactly as I had originally planned it (with the exception of bringing in David Wood). All the intense talk about Bernard Levin and balance turned out to be merely a smoke-screen to enable Wilson to get one of his most ardent supporters off a political programme. Whether Wilson was all along merely manoeuvring to achieve this curious result or whether he settled for it when he realized that his other objections were either impractical or unsubstantial, I have no way of knowing. A week later I received a letter from him dated 23 July 1963. It read:

Dear Milton,
Thank you for your letter of the 19th July. I am sorry I was not able to see the programme but I heard very favourable accounts of it from all who did. I wonder if you could kindly let me have the text?
Like you, I am sorry that there were difficulties in the early stages but I am sure that the changes made after the discussions had a lot to do with the programme's success.
Yours sincerely,
Harold Wilson.

It would be futile to speculate too deeply about the motives that inspired Harold Wilson and Transport House to indulge in this intricate and sustained bit of pressure over a programme that could have only minimal effect on Wilson's image and electoral chances. It probably began as resentment over Bernard Levin's presence on the programme, shifted ground in order to associate Wilson with some journalists he liked, and eventually settled for getting Barbara Castle off the air at a time when Wilson was trying to ingratiate himself with the right-wing and centre MPs of the Labour Party. Mrs Castle's appearance might have substantiated the view that Wilson was essentially a product of the party's left. At the time, he was eager to correct that impression.

Whatever the reasons were, the fact remains that a political leader was asserting his right to determine the shape and contents of a TV programme where, on any objective basis, no question of political imbalance ever existed. This right was something he would never have dared to demand of newspapers. The readiness with which some TV executives were prepared to accommodate his views must have been a gratifying experience for Wilson. In any case, incidents of interference by Transport House in TV programmes certainly proliferated during Wilson's years as Labour leader and Prime Minister. Resistance to this pressure tended to be stiffer in the BBC than amongst the commercial companies. The BBC, as we have seen, had a cherished tradition of independence from governmental influence. The commercial companies—smaller, more concerned with profits than principles, eager for a quiet life—tended to be more amenable and sensitive to politicians' complaints. It is this background of Wilson's obsession with how he and his party were treated on the box, his concern with the medium as a political persuader, and his disinterest in any of its other effects or manifestations, that explains a good deal of what happened to British broadcasting during Wilson's years of power.

During the 1964 election campaign Harold Wilson earned for himself a reputation as a master of media manipulation. His omnivorous reading of newspapers; his technical knowledge of newspaper production; his antennae for a good story, and his ability to get it reported with the maximum benefit for his party certainly impressed even the most cynical and experienced journalists. His cultivation of newspapermen, and their genuine appreciation of Wilson's frank and intimate treatment of them, was testified to by the gift of a set of books to Mr and Mrs Wilson by a group of journalists who had covered his campaign. This was an unusual gesture and evidence of a relationship between reporters and a party leader probably unique in British politics.[1]

During the campaign itself Wilson used television like an expert organist aware of the nuances of every pedal, lever, and stop. He was certain that politicians knew more about the use of the box than television experts. He demanded, but did not get, a television confrontation with Sir Alec Douglas-Home; he insisted that Labour's political party broadcasts did not use film which would give them an over-slick, professional air; he organized the timing of his public speeches so that whenever live television cameras were focused on him the most impressive aspects of the speech were transmitted.

Reporting on Wilson's method for making sure the most telling phrases in his speeches reached the air, Anthony Howard and Richard West wrote of his eve-of-poll speech at Liverpool,

> For the next five minutes he kept looking cautiously at his watch to judge the exact moment—9.16—when he was due to appear on a live ITN newscast. 'He'll be saying the bit about people,' said one of his party's television experts, and sure enough, at 9.16 sharp, Wilson paused and began to read out in a loud Churchillian tone: 'We care for people; they care for profit. We care about opportunity; they are pre-occupied with inheritance and conserving inheritance. . . .' A few minutes of this and Wilson relaxed again, until, at 9.24, a BBC man in the hall below leapt to wave his arms as a cue for another live broadcast. Once again Wilson's voice got louder and increasingly ponderous. This time he de-livered a call for a crusade.[2]

As a political leader fighting for power, Wilson had every right to use his understanding and grasp of the techniques of the medium to the best advantage of his party. If this meant manoeuvring for confrontation, manipulating speeches to make a better impression on the box, bargaining for every conceivable extra minute and benefit the television screen could give him, then this showed that he was aware, as so many of his rival politicians were not, of the potent new element that television had brought to the democratic electoral process.

More dubious, however, is the use of political power—whether by Government or Opposition—to cajole, bully, or menace television executives and producers so that the *content*, as distinguished from the *shape*, of a television programme will conform to the demands or desires of any particular politician or faction. The issue was summed up succinctly by Harford Thomas in *The Guardian*.

'These pressures are well known to journalists, and in a sense there is no harm in them,' wrote Mr Thomas. 'It is just part of the stock-in-trade of politics. The situation is somewhat different, though, in broadcasting where a statutory or quasi-constitutional requirement of impartiality is binding on the BBC and the ITV companies. The politician who tries to pressure a broadcast to his advantage is, as it were, compounding a felony. This being so, would it not be a useful convention for broadcasters always to make it known publicly when pressures of an improper kind have been brought to bear?'[3]

Although every political party has from time to time complained about the fairness of individual programmes, there is no doubt that Wilson and the Labour Party opposed the broadcasting authorities more frequently and more acrimoniously than any previous British Government. The incident I described at the beginning of this chapter was not reported at the time. It was only one of many such confrontations, eventually settled without fuss or publicity.

It is against this background of minor chivvying and bickering that the occasional reports of major rows between the television authorities and politicians must be assessed; for such niggling undermines television's political independence just as much as direct confrontation. Since Mr Wilson became its leader there is a depressingly long list of differences between those who run television and the Labour Party.

After thirteen years of Tory rule Labour came to power in 1964 with a tiny over-all majority of five. Governing on such a tightrope, it was perhaps predictable and forgiveable that the party should over-react to any broadcast that its leaders deemed to be against its interest. But over-react they certainly did. Most sensitive of the lot was Harold Wilson.

The tactics that we have already seen of objecting to the appearance on current affairs programmes of people whom Transport House or Harold Wilson found inconvenient, embarrassing, or undesirable were used more frequently and more successfully. Newspapers reported an increasing number of incidents where politicians or journalists were either neutralized or eased off programmes on which they were scheduled to appear.

Frequent targets for disapproval were the extreme left-wing MPs of the Labour Party. Since they were back-benchers, and not always in agreement with Government policy, television producers interested in achieving lively, provocative discussions were often tempted to invite the more articulate dissenters to participate in televised debates. This was particularly true of discussions of incomes policy, nuclear disarmament, Vietnam, where the left wing of the party strenuously opposed the Government line. Whenever pressure to have them taken off programmes was exerted, the so-called independent channel usually caved in. BBC resistance was much greater.

Thus in the summer of 1965, a planned discussion on Vietnam between the Tory MP, Lord Lambton, and the left-wing

Labour MP, J. J. Mendelson, was dropped from the commercial channel because of Labour's objections to Mr Mendelson's appearance.

That same summer when Ian Mikardo, another left-wing Labour MP, turned up at Rediffusion's studios to take part in a debate about nuclear disarmament with the Tory MP, Neil Marten, he was surprised to discover that a second Labour MP, Maurice Edelman, would be involved in the discussion. According to Walter Terry of the *Daily Mail*, the presence of Edelman was due to the insistence of Transport House who did not approve Mikardo's views on nuclear disarmament. They felt that Mr Edelman more accurately reflected the Government's case on this matter. In other words, the Labour Party felt that no political discussions between MPs should take place on TV without the presence of a Government representative to rebut any maverick or unorthodox opinions from awkward members of the left.

Bernard Levin, writing in the *Daily Mail*, commented on the Mendelson and Mikardo affair:

> These incidents merely highlight a growing scandal—the continued pressure on television by both political parties, and the continued acquiescence by television in this pressure.
>
> It is important to realize the nature of this pressure. It is not pressure on the companies and the BBC to put over Labour views against Conservative or vice versa. It is pressure on them to put on Labour views acceptable to the Labour heirarchy, and Conservative views likewise considered orthodox by Conservative leaders. . . .
>
> It is the selling of the pass by the BBC and the ITA (the ITA have behaved far worse than the BBC throughout) that has brought about the present lamentable state of affairs. . . . And once the pass was sold the enemy poured through, until we reached the present position, in which a telephone call from a Whips' office (it is grossly improper for the television authorities even to hold a conversation on such matters with such quarters) can—*and does*—result in the dropping of an item or the changing of its 'cast.' . . .
>
> Television has got to be fair. But I never yet heard that castration was the only cure for bias.[4]

A few months later, in October 1965, another row between Wilson's Government and the broadcasting authorities made generous headlines in the national press. This time it was the BBC that was to get the full blast of Labour disapproval. The grievances stemmed from the BBC's coverage of the Labour Party Conference at Blackpool. No less than five differences of opinion between the BBC and Transport House were reported at the time.

Adding a certain amount of zest to these clashes between the Labour Party and the BBC was a newspaper account that the Prime Minister himself had intervened in the argument by an angry dressing-down of a BBC executive in a hotel room in Blackpool. The incident, indeed, engendered enough political heat to stimulate a Tory MP to ask Mr Wilson a question about it in the Commons.

'Why was it that you misused your position at Blackpool during the Labour Party Conference to bully an employee of the BBC?' asked David Gibson-West, MP.

Mr Wilson denied that he had bullied anyone. He said that he had had one discussion—'not in an official capacity'—on the fact that the BBC had changed the rules about ministerial broadcasts. Whether the Prime Minister was bullying the BBC man or merely discussing some differences of opinion with him depends, I suppose, upon which chair you happen to be sitting on. But there was no doubt that sharp words were used in an atmosphere of hostility and recrimination. Certainly there were a number of sceptical voices raised in the Commons on hearing Mr Wilson's explanation. 'Your account of the incident,' said Sir Ian Orr-Ewing, another Tory MP, 'and other accounts, are at variance.'

Thus, only a year after attaining power, it was apparent that the Wilson Government was viewing the BBC with increasing irritation, annoyance, and suspicion. The Prime Minister himself was obviously contributing to this mood of exasperated disenchantment. Labour officials, indeed, did not hesitate to make their feelings known to the press. And they were dutifully reported.

'The Government and the Labour Party now seem firmly committed to an open and bitter clash with the BBC over allegations of a pro-Tory bias in its political programmes,' wrote Philip Rawsthorne in *The Guardian*. 'Labour leaders have now lathered themselves into such a fury of distrust that it seems only a thorough review of the situation by Sir Hugh Greene, the Director General, will satisfy them.'[5]

A few weeks later *The Sunday Times* Insight column had this to say: 'After the party's conference in Blackpool last month, the feelings had reached almost paranoid intensity. . . . Most television producers are frankly bewildered. Only a year ago they were being accused of leading a left-wing conspiracy

against the Conservatives—now the accusation has been turned
inside out. But the continuous sniping is having its inevitable
effect on morale.'6

Whatever else might be said about Wilson's first term as
Prime Minister, it cannot be said that he was unconcerned
about television. He quibbled, fretted, argued, plotted about it
to an inordinate degree. But his concern about broadcasting
was strictly confined to achieving for himself and his party
what he considered to be the most advantageous use of air
time. Nothing else. When, in 1966, after almost a year and a
half of power, Wilson called a new election, his Government
could look back on the decisions it had taken about television
itself and its dealings with issues such as the introduction of
colour and the increase of the BBC licence fee, and chalk up
a massive zero.

A month later, Harold Wilson was back in Downing Street
with a healthy majority of ninety-seven. On the very day of
his triumph, Wilson continued his peculiar vendetta against
the BBC. After the BBC and ITV had competed with each
other by extensive coverage of the polling results in the early
morning of 1 April 1966 the obvious climax to their broadcasts
was to be an interview with the victorious Prime Minister.
Both networks wanted a live, informal chat with him as he
travelled down from Liverpool by train after his grand victory.
The BBC had gone to considerable trouble to convert a special
coach of the train into a mobile studio so that this pioneering
television job—i.e. a live broadcast from a moving train—could
be accomplished under the best technical conditions. But
Wilson deliberately humiliated the Corporation by refusing to
talk to the BBC reporter on the train. Nor would he take part
in a question-and-answer session with Robin Day who was to
contact him by television link from a BBC London studio.To
make the snub even more pointed, Wilson granted an interview
to an ITV reporter on the same train, describing his feelings on
that heady morning and some of his future intentions.

The official explanation, subsequently given to the press, for
this refusal to co-operate with the nation's most important network on this significant occasion was that the BBC had omitted
to make a formal application to Transport House for such an
interview. Wilson had known about the BBC's plan only two
days before the election, when he had read about it in a newspaper. The clear innuendo underlying this extraordinary rebuff
was that if the BBC refused to obey protocol, Mr Wilson was
determined to teach them a lesson.

During the 1966 election campaign, hypersensitivity about television amongst broadcasting executives and politicians achieved at times both ludicrous and hysterical proportions. There was a BBC decision to postpone—later rescinded—a children's puppet show starring two singing pigs, Pinky and Perky. The programme was called 'You, too, can be a Prime Minister,' and someone was afraid it might be taking a party line. The average age of viewers for the Pinky-Perky show would be about six. There was some fretting, too, at Transport House, about the broadcasting of the American spy fantasy, *The Man From Uncle*, on election night. Presumably they felt that more potential Labour voters than Tory would prefer the delights of this preposterous programme to doing their duty at the ballot box.

In the month before polling day there was hardly a morning when one could open one's paper and not find a prominent story discussing some argument, some manoeuvre, some apprehension, about the way television was being used. It was clear from the rude rebuff he gave to the BBC on the election train, that Harold Wilson was extremely irritated and angry over this running battle with the Corporation.

Thus, looking back at this record of squabbles, there can be no doubt that there was a distinct atmosphere of chilly hostility, to put it mildly, between Wilson and the BBC when Labour returned to power in 1966. Indicative, perhaps, of the Prime Minister's true concern about broadcasting—except in the narrow field of political balance—was the readiness with which he was prepared to switch and change his Postmasters General.

The keen young Anthony Wedgwood Benn, who managed to make no major decisions about television during his term of office, was replaced by the colourless Edward Short who, in two years of office, made only one—authorizing the introduction of colour. Mr Short in April 1968 was replaced by Roy Mason who, after barely nine months in the job and without making a single important decision about broadcasting, was replaced by John Stonehouse.

The constant drip of grouses and complaints from governmental quarters was bound to undermine in some measure the confidence of some of the BBC's executives, particularly those most closely associated with current affairs programmes. But if there was an edgy nervousness about how Transport House might react to what the Corporation transmitted, it had not fundamentally changed the basic pattern of independence that the BBC had always claimed as its right. After almost three years of Wilson's Government there were still satire shows on the BBC tilting irreverently at political figures including the Prime Minister himself. There was a comedy series called *Till Death Us Do Part* which launched the most repulsive specimen of the working-class ever seen anywhere on television. Alf Garnett, although a Tory voter, reflected the ugliest under-side of those very people the Labour Party depended upon for its support. There was not a tittle of evidence that Sir Hugh Greene, the BBC's Director General, had been in any way over-awed or affected by Government pressure; the BBC's coverage of contemporary events showed no compromise of its usual standards of objective and forthright comment.

Thus, except for creating an atmosphere of sulky ill-will between the Government and the Corporation, three years of niggling harrassment had not changed things fundamentally. But on 14 June 1967 Harold Wilson was suddenly presented with an opportunity to make a personal and significant impact upon the shape and future of British broadcasting. Lord Normanbrook, Chairman of the Board of Governors of the BBC, had died.

Lord Normanbrook, who had been secretary to the Cabinet for fifteen years and head of Britain's Civil Service from 1956 to 1962, had been made the BBC Chairman in April 1964 by the Tory Prime Minister Harold Macmillan.

During Lord Normanbrook's chairmanship the BBC broke through into its most turbulent, controversial, and adventurous phase. But it was not so much Lord Normanbrook's presence, as the influence of the Director General, Sir Hugh Greene, that encouraged the BBC to engage in its questioning of revered institutions and beliefs.

Lord Normanbrook's contribution to this questing mood within the BBC was chiefly one of non-intervention. Ever since Reith's day, the Director General had been in firm control of the day-to-day execution of policy, with the Chairman and his Board of Governors merely acting as a supervisory body ensur-ing that the broad principles of broadcasting, as laid down by Parliament and the Charter, were carried out. When, however, the dominating personality of Reith had left the BBC, succeed-ing Chairmen had tried to reduce the influence of the Director General over BBC affairs. Sir Ernest Simon, as Chairman in 1947, had complained that the activities of the Governors, except for the Chairman, were confined to 'reading papers and attending Board meetings.'[7]

Indeed, the question of who manipulated the 'real' power at the BBC—the Chairman or the Director General—has never been very satisfactorily answered. Constitutionally, there is no doubt that the ultimate responsibility for the BBC resides with the Chairman and his Board of Governors. 'It is in them that the authority is vested,' said the Pilkington Report. 'It is they who are answerable for performance; it is they who must preserve the independence of broadcasting.'[8]

But historically it has been the Director General who has wielded true power in the Corporation. There have been three main reasons for the Director General's dominance. First, he is a full-time professional in charge of full-time officials, while the Governors are recruited on a part-time basis with a short-term tenure, usually five years. Second, the sheer size of the BBC operation—four radio channels, two TV channels, the overseas broadcasts, a host of supplementary activities like publishing and programme sales—makes it impossible for the Governors to become intimately involved with the day-to-day activities of the largest broadcasting institution in the world. Third, Reith's gigantic personality firmly set the pattern of control within the Corporation by which the Governors' responsibilities were accepted as merely general and supervisory, rather than particular and executive, and that within an agreed policy of fiscal and programming matters, the Director General was granted almost total independence to get on with the job.

This power of the Director General has naturally irked Governments. 'Another curious thing about the BBC,' wrote Reginald Bevins, a Tory Postmaster General in Macmillan's Government, 'is the apparent inability of the BBC Governors to exercise any real influence. . . . They ought to be the governing body. It always seemed to me they were governed by professionals.'[9]

The Pilkington Committee emphasized the need for the Governors to act in a critical capacity within the Corporation and to stimulate and curb the professionals when necessary. 'They must see the service "from the outside,"' said the 1962 Report. 'Their task is to be thoroughly aware of public opinion in all its variety, to care about it, and take proper and full account of it. Having done so, they must then identify the public interest in broadcasting, defined as the fullest possible realization of the purposes of broadcasting, and secure it through the control of the executive arm.'[10]

The Pilkington Committee also emphasized another serious

responsibility of the Governors: the preservation of the independence of the Corporation. 'Just as they must keep their executive arm sensitive to significant opinion which might otherwise not make itself felt, so they must ensure that their executive arm does not, to the detriment of the purposes of broadcasting, give way to pressures simply because they can make themselves felt. *Most obviously they must be ready to resist direct or indirect intervention by the Government in programming.*'[11] (My italics.)

In spite of these misgivings, definitions, and assertions by Postmasters General, the Beveridge and Pilkington Committees, and the BBC Chairmen, it was indisputable that the image, the direction, and the philosophy of the BBC was in all important essentials determined by the personality of the Director General rather than the views of the Chairman or the Governors. What the BBC had become up to the moment of Lord Normanbrook's death in 1967 was due to the inspiration and vision of Directors General like Lord Reith, Sir William Haley, Sir Hugh Greene, rather than Chairmen like Lord Clarendon, J. H. Whitley, Lord Simon, Sir Arthur fforde, or Lord Normanbrook.

No doubt the process of shifting power from the BBC professionals to the Governors appointed by Royal Charter was slowly gathering momentum as the range and significance of broadcasting grew. Television, added to radio, bestowed upon the Director General of the BBC a near-monopoly position in the dissemination of news, opinions, and values which was bound to rouse misgivings. Was it wise to allow one strong man to hold in his hands the apparatus for shaping society so significantly? Shouldn't there be another strong man, in the post of Chairman, to act as a counter-weight to such individual power?

Such a proposition would obviously have its attractions for a man like Harold Wilson, whose years of government had been bedevilled by a running guerrilla war between his officials and the BBC. What was needed was someone in control of the BBC who would have a sympathetic understanding of the position of Governments and political parties when they were faced by a recalcitrant or obstinate Director General or BBC executive who refused to see their point of view. What was needed was a man with the experience and the will to override the Director General if necessary. What was needed was a demonstration to the BBC that a Government could, in the last analysis, cut them down to size by determining who was going to be their real boss. Harold Wilson may not have had all or any of these considerations in mind when, towards the end of July 1967, he appointed Lord Hill of Luton Chairman of the BBC. But that was the way it certainly looked to a lot of people that summer.

It was at a cocktail party on the evening of 25 July 1967 that an indiscreet guest divulged a juicy morsel of gossip. Officially the information he revealed was scheduled for release to the press a few days later. The name of the indiscreet informant was Harold Wilson.

'He was obviously in great good humour,' wrote Stuart Hood, a former BBC Controller of TV, describing the incident. 'Indeed, at one point in the evening he was unable to contain his satisfaction with himself any longer and, approaching a well-known television performer, said to him affably, rib-nudgingly: "I have done something the BBC won't like." What this naughtiness was the Prime Minister at this point kept *in petto* but as the evening wore on the need to communicate his prank became too strong for him. Seeking out the same guest, he revealed that he had appointed Lord Hill to be Chairman of the BBC.'[12]

Such a leak could not be kept very long from the quivering ears of Fleet Street. Awkward questions were soon being asked. The public announcement had to be rushed into print. The next day, Wednesday 26 July, Robert Lusty, the BBC's Acting Chairman, was sent for by the Postmaster General, Edward Short. He was told that in just three hours' time, at eight o'clock that very evening, an announcement would be made about the BBC's new Chairman. He would be taking over his duties at the beginning of September.

According to the version of this meeting given by Kenneth Adam, the BBC's Director of Television from 1961 to 1968, the Postmaster General met Mr Lusty surrounded by officials and in a state of high embarrassment.

' "Charles Smith is to be your next Chairman," were the Postmaster General's first words, and he had to be corrected by one of his officials. "Hill, sir, Hill." '[13]

There was no doubt in Lusty's mind that the Postmaster General was completely unaware of the impact that this appointment would make at the BBC. Judging from his slip about Hill's name, it seems likely that Short had been only briefly consulted by the Prime Minister about the selection— assuming there had been any consultation at all.

'The Postmaster General seemed completely unaware of the difficulty in which this sudden decision placed the BBC in general and me in particular,' said Lusty in an interview he gave to *The Times*. 'The ITA, as its chief competitor, is not wholly beloved by the BBC, and to have its Chief translated in this way was a bombshell and I knew that I would somehow have to achieve a dampening of the inevitable explosion. Of all this the Postmaster General seemed oblivious. It was a Government appointment and that was that. It should be accepted without question or doubt.'[14]

Asked about rumours that Hill's appointment was an attempt by the Government to discipline the BBC's 'sharpshooters,' Lusty replied, 'I think the appointment must have significance. It was too strange a one not to have. But I would very much doubt if it had much to do with programmes. My personal view is that it illustrates the total inability of the Government to recognize the differing natures and conceptions of the BBC and the ITA.'[15]

When that same evening, at a hurriedly assembled meeting of the BBC's Board of Management, Sir Hugh Greene flatly told his chief executives that 'Charlie Hill of the ITA' was to be their new Chairman, disbelief and consternation was their reaction. According to Kenneth Adam, Greene asked if he should resign. But the protests of his colleagues, and the possibility of a mass walk-out if he went, restrained him. The meeting broke up in a cloud of gloom, as the executives went off to partake of a previously arranged dinner being given for Anthony Barber, the recently appointed Chairman of the Conservative Party.

'After the wild strawberries, and over the port, someone said: "The condemned men ate a hearty dinner,"' wrote Kenneth Adam. 'It was a macabre evening, and at the end of it, we were not certain Greene would stay.'[16]

Sir Hugh Greene, however, did stay. But not for very long. Just a year later, in July 1968, he announced his decision to retire at the comparatively youthful age of fifty-eight. Since normal retirement age at the BBC is sixty, it had been assumed that he would carry on as Director General until November 1970. But personal reasons (he was being divorced from his wife) and perhaps a feeling that his usefulness at the BBC had been diminished in the new atmosphere attendant on Lord Hill's presence as Chairman, probably influenced his decision to go. Even then he did not sever all his connections with the BBC. He was made one of the BBC's twelve Governors—the first Director General to take that position. But this appointment did not last out its full five years. In August 1971, because of 'business commitments,' Sir Hugh resigned as a BBC Governor.

In passing, it might also be mentioned that at the same time as he appointed Lord Hill as Chairman, Harold Wilson also decided to raise the number of BBC Governors from nine to twelve. Since this was done against the advice of the BBC hierarchy, it was another issue provoking suspicion and resentment between the Corporation and the Prime Minister.

In terms of simple protocol, it can be seen that the manner in which Harold Wilson foisted Lord Hill on to the BBC was brusque, insulting, and deliberately provocative. Coming as it did after a history of petty squabbling and unfounded accusations of a political imbalance which loomed large only in the eyes of the Prime Minister and his immediate clique, it was bound to arouse all sorts of misgivings about the Government's real intentions.

'There is reason for real public concern over the circumstances of Mr Wilson's appointment of Lord Hill as Chairman of the BBC but this has nothing to do with Lord Hill's political past nor with his performance as Chairman of the ITA,' thundered a leader in *The Sunday Times*. '. . . The real cause for alarm arises first because the Chairman of the BBC and of the ITA are two entirely different sorts of officials and secondly from the fact that the BBC should have such dark doubts about Mr Wilson's motives in making this appointment. . . . The worries at Broadcasting House are understandable not because of anything Lord Hill has done or is likely to do, but because of Mr Wilson's suspected motives in appointing him. The Prime Minister has had a prolonged unhappy relationship with the BBC and with its producers almost since Labour first took office. In contrast he has had a good relationship with the ITA and with the companies. . . . The existence of the present outburst of anger and anxiety at the BBC reflects a lamentable relationship between the Prime Minister and the Corporation which has never existed under any previous Government.'[17]

Coming to the same sombre conclusion as *The Sunday Times* was David Haworth in a full page article in *The Observer*. 'It seems plain that Mr Wilson intends Lord Hill to rein in the Corporation and head it in a different direction—using a whip if necessary. He may have picked the very man for the job,' wrote Mr Haworth.

'As for the BBC, it's Hill's political experience that the staff fear most. Few people in the Corporation are suggesting that, as a Conservative ex-Minister, he might play party politics in

his new post; but it is widely suspected that a man so imbued
with politics will be particularly sensitive to nods and winks
from No. 10. This is why one BBC man describes the Hill
appointment as "Harold's revenge" for the way the Government has suffered in the Prime Minister's view, at the hands of
the BBC—this has annoyed the Prime Minister even more than
his treatment by the Press.'[18]

Indeed, the more one examines the background of Wilson's
decision to ask Lord Hill to head the BBC, the more curious
the appointment becomes. As baffled as anyone by this move
was Lord Hill of Luton himself. He had been given no hint or
warning that he was being considered for the post. The deed
itself was accomplished by a two-sentence telephone conversation. 'I think you have done a very good job as head of the
ITV,' said the Prime Minister. 'Would you like to take over
the BBC?' Hill, pausing only long enough to recover from his
astonishment, immediately accepted.

Charles Hill, who was born in 1904 the son of a piano-
maker, floated into the top reaches of the English Establishment
through his ability as an administrator and his astuteness in
public relations. His formal education was achieved largely
through scholarships which took him through grammar school
and Cambridge, where he studied medicine. After a few years
as a practising doctor, he found administration more attractive
and became Secretary of the British Medical Association. In
this capacity, he shared the headlines with Aneurin Bevan as
they fought each other over the details of how doctors should
be treated in the new National Health Service.

But it was his fruity, rich, reassuring voice as the BBC's
Radio Doctor that brought him national fame. Bright and
early in the morning, he dispensed in five-minute, weekly
doses practical advice about the ramifications of the liver and
the subtleties of constipation. His broadcasting technique was
chummy and down-to-earth and best designed to appeal to the
common man sitting on the loo. Through the voices of characters like Sam Stomach, Bert Bowel, Truman Testicle, and
Dierdre Duodenum he took his listeners on mysterious trips
through the alimentary canal and other parts of the body.

'This is stomach speaking. Yes, I mean it, *your* stomach,' said
Lord Hill on Boxing Day 1949, in what he describes as his
favourite programme. 'In fact, I'm the shop-steward of the
Society of Suffering Stomachs. As a rule I get on with my job
without as much as a murmur or rumble. But I've got something to say this morning. Yesterday—Christmas Day—you

bullied me. . . . Down the chute they came: sweet after sweet, nut after nut, biscuits, oranges. . . . If there is anything that upsets me it's sweet things between meals. I had my own back, mind you: those who sent down lashings of lollipops, I didn't leave them much appetite for dinner. You can't stuff me with sweets and then tackle me with turkey, for I won't have it. . . .'[19]

But Charles Hill's promising prophylactic career was cut short by his election as the Conservative MP for Luton in 1950. There followed a series of Government posts—Parliamentary Secretary to the Ministry of Food, Postmaster General, Chancellor of the Duchy of Lancaster, Minister of Housing—until he was ruthlessly dismissed from office by Prime Minister Macmillan in the Cabinet purge of 1962.

He has been described as the typical organization man with tastes that are middlebrow, ambitions that are middle-class, and views that hew resolutely down the middle line of every issue and every problem. His avuncular charm, his cherubic face, his air of sympathetic reasonableness mask a shrewd mind and an instinctive acceptance of the side that will cause the least trouble. He is eager, too, to disavow any suggestion of ruthlessness or personal ambition. He likes to think of his ever-present pipe and his rumpled suit as irrefutable evidence of his basic humility. 'For me, every meeting throughout the five and a half years I was a Cabinet Minister was something of an occasion,' he has written in his autobiography. 'I could not get over my surprise that I was there at all.'[20]

One day, without any warning, he was called into Macmillan's office and told that his euphoric days in the Cabinet were over. The Prime Minister wanted to make way for newer and younger men. About a year later there was another sudden reversal of his fortunes. He was invited to become a life peer on the understanding that he would soon become the next, and third, Chairman of the Independent Television Authority.[21] In June 1963, the announcement was made.

By Labour politicians the appointment was greeted with a cry of apopletic fury. Lord Morrison of Lambeth in the Lords made a vitriolic attack of almost unprecedented abuse against both the method of the appointment and the competence of Lord Hill of Luton for the post.

I cannot say less than that I think it is a public scandal. We were chivvied about 'jobs for the boys' by the Conservative Party in the Commons when the boards were being set up for the publicly owned industries. It was not true. . . .

But if ever there was a job for a boy, my Lords, it is this one. . . . It is a party appointment and it is a job where that kind of suspicion ought not to exist. I do not say that no politician should ever be considered for a post of this kind. It depends on the politician, although there is a lot to be said for his not being a politician. It is no good for the reputation of our country or the uprightness of our public administration that this kind of thing should take place . . . the whole thing smells from beginning to end. . . . It is shameful. . . .[22]

Lord Francis-Williams in the same debate said that the appointment was regrettable. He thought it was the first time in the history of broadcasting in this country, whether by BBC or by commercial television, that the Chairman of either authority had been a party political man.[23]

And two days later in the Commons a Labour MP indicated his displeasure at Lord Hill's appointment by asking Mr Macmillan to comment on the fact that 'There is great concern that Lord Hill, whom the Prime Minister did not think good enough for his Cabinet a year ago, should be appointed.' The name of the politician who made that observation was Harold Wilson.[24]

It is obvious that in 1963 Lord Hill hardly lived up to the Labour Party's concept of an ideal figure to guide, influence, and lead commercial television. What had changed, one might reasonably ask, what had Lord Hill achieved in his four years at the ITA so that a Labour Prime Minister—a man who had himself questioned Hill's fitness for the job— should have decided to promote him to the much more influential, much more prestigious task of heading the BBC? What criteria was Wilson using when he told Hill that he had done 'a very good job' as head of commercial television?

Sift through the record as diligently as one can, it is difficult to find the evidence that convinced Harold Wilson that here was the best man in the nation to take charge of the most powerful communications organization in Britain, if not the world. What had he actually done?

In the programme field his record was at best negative and at worst abysmal. If his presence at the ITA was in some measure designed to improve the quality of the variety shows, quizzes, soap operas, adventure series that dominated the commercial network, particularly at peak time, it singularly failed to have the slightest effect.

Indeed, on the very eve of his appointment to the BBC, only three months before he was congratulated by Wilson for doing a 'very good job,' the programme side of ITV was pursuing its usual line of dogged mediocrity.

'There are times when you feel that Channel 9 no longer cares,' I wrote in the *Evening Standard* on 5 April 1967. 'Their schedules take on the look of a gravy-stained menu at a hamburger joint on the verge of bankruptcy. Every item is old. Every item is predictable. Every item signals a weary contempt for the customer.'

Other commentators at the time may have been more restrained in their expressions of resignation or disgust about the general level of commercial television, but the basic refrain was very much the same. I doubt if there is a single serious television critic who would support the view that four years of Lord Hill's chairmanship had changed in any significant way the monotony and dreariness of the bulk of ITV programmes.

It is true that just before Lord Hill was catapulted to higher things there were some rumours that the ITA was taking a sterner line about the quality of programmes. It was his support—against vigorous opposition from some of the programme contractors—that resulted in a regular half-hour news programme by the Independent Television News every night at ten o'clock.

If Lord Hill's contribution to the programme side of commercial television was minimal, what else had he done to catch Wilson's approving eye? In the administrative field, his most signal and significant act was the reshaping of the structure of the commercial network in June 1967. Since the old franchises had expired, it was Hill's responsibility to choose the contractors who would be given fresh six-year contracts. With the addition of a new region—Yorkshire—there were fifteen companies to be selected instead of the fourteen which were the basis of the original geographical arrangement. It had been confidently assumed that the ITA would renew the franchises of the existing companies. There might be a little jiggling here and there of responsibilities to be allotted to the old companies, but no one expected a serious change. But Lord Hill surprised everyone— newspapers, TV authorities, financiers—by ruthlessly removing three of the companies from their controlling positions and by giving commercial TV franchises to three entirely new companies.

This drastic step, which was a humiliating rebuff to the three major established companies in that it offered them only

minority interests in the companies they had hitherto controlled, certainly demonstrated that Lord Hill was not the
paper tiger some had assumed him to be.[25]

But as we shall see in more detail in the next chapter, there
was little about this radical reorganization—either in the
manner in which it was done, the reasons for doing it, or
in its ultimate consequences—that warrants much praise for
efficiency or far-sightedness. *The Times*, for example, with
reference to this phase of Lord Hill's career, said, 'his final
decisions at the ITA had not shown good judgment. The
redistribution of contracts was carried out without adequate
thought about the financial consequences. . . . There is not
yet enough evidence to establish whether the new contractors
will be any better than the old.'[26] In the event, *The Times*'s
scepticism was fully vindicated. The new contractors turned
out to be no better than the old.

Thus, peer as one will at Lord Hill's record as Chairman of
the ITA—the negative impact he had on programming policy
and the almost farcical results of his dramatic reallotment of
contracts—there is a decided dearth of evidence to explain
why Harold Wilson thought Hill was the right man to lead
the BBC in an era when its influence might have significant
repercussions on the shape and conduct of the nation's affairs.

It does not, however, take much perception to guess what
aspects of Hill's career and personality made him so clearly
Wilson's choice for the job. In his four years at the ITA, Hill
had undoubtedly proved he could get along with the Prime
Minister. There had been a few rows about political balance
and unfairness but they had always been neatly resolved and
swept into the out-tray with a minimum of fuss. The BBC, on
the other hand, had succeeded time and time again in ruffling
the Prime Minister's feathers over its insistence that the Labour
Party and the Government had no business tinkering over the
details of broadcasting affairs. It was reasonable to assume
that what Lord Hill had done at the ITA, he could do at the
BBC. Could he not more efficiently oil the channels of communication between the Labour Party and Broadcasting
House? Would he not restrain the irritating assumption of
some of the BBC's young hawks that politicians were fair game
for satire and ridicule? Would he not understand the politician's
language and be more responsive to their needs?

For his own good reasons, therefore, Harold Wilson chose
Lord Hill of Luton. Constitutionally the Prime Minister is
answerable to no one when he selects the Chairman of either

of the broadcasting authorities—the BBC or the ITA. He is under no compulsion to consult anyone, to explain anything, to provide any reasons when making his choice. Because the nature and importance of broadcasting have changed so much since this procedure was established, it is worth examining briefly the background and consequences of the present constitutional position.

When the BBC was given its Royal Charter in 1927, it could not possibly have been foreseen just how powerful a role broadcasting would eventually have in the life of the nation. Under that Charter, the King-in-Council—which in effect meant the Prime Minister of the day—was given the right to appoint the BBC Governors and their Chairman. Since the idea of turning the BBC into a public corporation under a Royal Charter was primarily Reith's, it can be assumed that it was never envisaged that the BBC's Chairman would be a political appointment or that he might conceivably challenge the power of the Director General within the Corporation.

As we have already seen, successive Chairmen of the BBC had begun to chafe at their restricted functions. All the circumstances surrounding Lord Hill's appointment indicate that it was definitely Harold Wilson's intention that the power seesaw within the Corporation should be weighted even more decisively in the Chairman's favour.

Hill's background as a former Cabinet Minister and his experience at the ITA equipped him admirably for just such a take-over.

If, then, the Chairman of the BBC was to become a more dominant—if not *the* dominant figure in the Corporation's hierarchical structure—was it right that so significant an appointment should be left solely to the discretion of the Prime Minister? Was it ever intended that the real power to control broadcasting—and by his right to select the heads of both the BBC and the ITA the Prime Minister has such power—should be exclusively in the hands of the Prime Minister, as his personal prerogative, to be exercised with reference to no one?

Prime Ministers before the war clearly did not think that they had been given such a right. Both Ramsey Macdonald and Neville Chamberlain canvassed a large section of informed opinion—including that of the broadcasting authorities themselves—before choosing their BBC Chairman. Reith may not have always agreed with their choice, but he was well aware of what was going on behind the scenes.[27]

Post-war Prime Ministers, too, took part in an elaborate consultative process with people like the Postmaster General, the Director General at the Post Office, and the Head of the Civil Service, before choosing BBC Chairmen. When Sir Alec Douglas-Home gave Lord Normanbrook the job, he informed the leader of the Opposition, Harold Wilson, of his intention. Wilson had no objections.

Like so many areas of British constitutional practice, there was no clearly formulated procedure for the Prime Minister's selection of the BBC Chairman. Yet however vague the terms of selection, it is quite clear that Prime Ministers before Harold Wilson accepted advice before they made their choices. But in the case of Lord Hill, there is no evidence that Wilson spoke to anyone of any significance about what he was up to. When one examines the list of people Harold Wilson might have consulted about transferring Lord Hill from the ITA to the BBC, it is hard to imagine any of them being enthusiastic about the Prime Minister's curious decision. Since consultation might only arouse opposition, why bother to consult?

Thus not only had Harold Wilson broken tradition by putting a professional politician into a job which considered and concerned opinion had always insisted should not be held by a politician, but he had done it without regard to any consultative procedure that had hitherto been followed. Without any serious Parliamentary discussion or argument, Wilson had succeeded in enlarging the already generous power of personal patronage possessed by a Prime Minister so that it now enabled him to decide which personalities should control and oversee the most influential medium of communication in the land. The only restraint on the consequences of his choice was the doctrine—also suitably vague—that the broadcasting authorities were always to be independent of Government. We have already seen how varied in the mind of a Government are the definitions of the word 'independent.' While Wilson in appointing Lord Hill may have only been seeking someone who he instinctively felt would share his views of the limits of BBC 'independence,' what was there to prevent some future, more unscrupulous Prime Minister choosing a Chairman for more obvious, and even sinister, political and social purposes?

Harold Wilson's final move in completing the politicians' take-over of British broadcasting was his appointment of Herbert Bowden, now Lord Aylestone, to replace Lord Hill at the Independent Television Authority. A dour, hard-headed politician, Aylestone was Labour's Chief Whip for many years and eventually became Leader of the House of Commons. His appointment was a blatant affirmation of Wilson's theory that broadcasting was too important to be left to anyone but politicians.

If politicians were unconcerned about this monopolization of the top broadcasting posts by politicians, some serious independent commentators were not so complacent. Ivan Yates wrote in *The Observer*,

> Mr Bowden is a man of almost old-fashioned probity, conventional, self-disciplined, a stickler for the proprieties.... There need be no fears of party political bias. Both Bowden and Lord Hill would lean over backwards rather than favour their former party colleagues. The question mark raised by the pattern of these appointments is simply that both men will be called on from time to time to deal with complaints by politicians against their natural enemies, journalistic commentators and critics—as well as television producers. Wouldn't they be less than human if sometimes they were inclined to entertain the politicians' objections a little too readily?
>
> Politicians sometimes think television and radio are intended to be just platforms for them. But they are, of course, also media for investigating and exposing their records and pretensions. The difference in role between politicians and the journalists who carry out these tasks contains an element of necessary conflict. . . .[28]

Professor E. G. Wedell, Secretary of the ITA from 1961 to 1964 and now Professor of Adult Education at the University of Manchester, voiced similar misgivings:

> It would be regrettable if the chairmanship of the broadcasting organizations were to come to be regarded as the exclusive preserve of politicians. Politics is only a part of broadcasting, and not the most important. Nor is our public life so deficient in men and women of ability that politicians have to be called in to fill the breach. More important, since the whole point of interposing public corporations between governments and the producers is to remove the day-to-day control of broadcasting out of the political arena, it is dangerous to attenuate this distinction. It is not sufficient to balance an appointment from the Right with one from the Left, since politicians of all parties have certain interests in common, which may well not coincide with those of their constituents

who are the effective clients of the broadcasting organizations. . . . It is dangerous to have at the head of the broadcasting organizations people who may have too much
sympathy with the politicians' need of a favourable image.[29]

What, then, has happened to British broadcasting under the
regime of Lord Hill and Lord Aylestone? Has it become better
or worse? Has it become less or more mature? Less or more
responsible? Less or more courageous, adventurous, concerned? Were the critics justified in suspecting that broadcasting would become less critical, less sceptical, less abrasive in
its approach to politicians? Was television a more respected
medium than it had been before and was there evidence that
under the guidance of Lords Hill and Aylestone the direction
of television was set firmly on a path that was good for both
broadcasting and the nation? We shall see.

CHAPTER III

THE FRANCHISE SCANDAL

You can talk about the goldrush, you can talk of forty-nine
Or the pirates that the Caribbean sail;
You can talk about the Yukon, but if once the choice were mine
I'd pack my bags and ride the franchise trail.

This ballad, sung in the twangy rhythms of an American folk song, set the mood of Nemone Lethbridge's play, 'The Franchise Trail.' It was scheduled to be seen late in July 1968 on the first night's programming of a new British television company, London Weekend Television. No one can deny the audacity of the thinking that planned to present such a play on such a night. For 'The Franchise Trail' was a bold, cynical farcical romp, based upon the vulgar and avaricious process that had resulted in London Weekend itself becoming the surprised possessor of one of the most lucrative television contracts in Britain.*

To understand how London Weekend acquired this contract, one has to go back a bit. When the original contracts were handed out to the fourteen television companies, they were all meant to expire in July 1964. Although the earliest companies took to the air in 1955 and some of the smaller companies did not start to broadcast until 1961, they were all legally dead in July 1964 unless the ITA renewed their licences.[1] This the Authority did. Just before the expiration of these contracts the Authority advertised for fresh groups to take on the franchises. Under Lord Hill's chairmanship, the Authority interviewed twenty-two groups who had applied for these valuable slices of the commercial television bonanza. None of the new consortia was wanted. Lord Hill announced that he was quite happy with the status quo: there were to be no changes and all the existing companies would continue in business.

However, due to the possibility that commercial television might soon change from its 405- to a 625-line definition standard, and to a hint from the Conservative Government that it might authorize a second commercial channel, the

---

* Due to a technician's strike and other problems 'The Franchise Trail' was transmitted, not on opening night, but a few weeks later.

Authority decided that the renewed contracts would last for
only three years instead of the contemplated six. By 1966 it was
clear that the uncertainty about the future of commercial
television had not been resolved, and the companies were
granted another year's extension until July 1968.

On 21 December 1966, when it became clear that the
second commercial channel would not be possible for some
time, Lord Hill invited applications for new franchises.

The frenzied scramble that followed Lord Hill's invitation
was a genteel British version of such other financial stampedes
as the gold rush in Alaska, the uranium panic in Canada, and
the nickel dash in Australia.

Financiers made their calculations. Accountants used their
slide rules. Brokers made their soundings. It was apparent to
all that here was money, money, money.

Everyone piled in on the act—merchant bankers, lawyers,
trade unions, newspapers, magazines, circuses, insurance
companies, refrigerator manufacturers, actors, co-ops. The
only thing that many of them had in common was that they
knew nothing about television and couldn't care a fig about its
history, its purpose, or its future.

Newspapers like the *Daily Telegraph*, the *Yorkshire Post*, *The
Observer*, *The Scotsman*; politicians like Jo Grimond, former head
of the Liberal Party, Maurice Macmillan, MP, Aidan Crawley,
MP; publishers like Penguin, Collins, Weidenfeld; actors like
Richard Burton, Stanley Baker, Richard Attenborough;
journals like the *New Statesman*, *The Spectator*; companies like
Bowater Paper, General Electric, EMI, Decca, ICI; pension
funds like those of Imperial Tobacco and Harvey's of Bristol;
bankers, insurance companies, and brokers like Lombard
Banking, Pearl Assurance, Samuel Montague; peers of the
realm like Lord Harlech, Lord Goodman, and Lord Riverdale;
impressarios, journalists, and entertainers like Peter Bridge,
John Freeman, John Morgan, David Frost; even academic
foundations like Magdalen College, Oxford, and University
College, London, were but a fraction of the institutions,
businesses, and individuals who grouped themselves together
in a number of consortia awaiting Lord Hill's approval and
benefice.

What these groups were now bidding for were fifteen contracts instead of the original fourteen. This meant that there
would now be five companies, instead of four, with access to
large population areas—two in London and one each in the
Midlands, Lancashire, and Yorkshire. The other ten regional

companies—smaller both in scope and potential—would remain unchanged.

When all the bids were in on 15 April 1967, thirty-six groups had applied to the ITA for the fifteen available franchises. In the four months between the announcement for applications and the closing of the bids, the competing consortia jostled and conspired like medieval barons as they tried to shape themselves into images that might appeal to Lord Hill and his twelve ITA Governors. Since all these new groups had to establish, besides their other credentials, the ability actually to transmit programmes, it was necessary to include in their teams individuals familiar with the technical and administrative problems of the medium. The best of these were naturally already employed with the BBC and the independent TV companies. Furtive, secret alliances and understandings had, therefore, to be made between some of the new consortia and the TV executives willing to join them should they get the contracts.

'Eighteen top TV executives visited the Independent Television Authority's headquarters in cloak and dagger style yesterday,' was how a *Daily Mirror* reporter described the atmosphere in which interviews of the new applicants were taking place. 'They were attending the first interview for the groups which have applied to run the new Yorkshire ITV station.

'The executives—from the BBC and ITV companies—entered and left the offices in Brompton Road, Knightsbridge, by the back door. They refused to be photographed. For they do not want their employers to know yet that they are associated with the bids to run the new channels due to open in July 1968.'[2]

While some of the consortia were organized with the precision of a military operation, others almost stumbled into existence. It was at the regular weekly noisy lunch in a Soho pub held by the satirical magazine *Private Eye*, that journalist and TV commentator John Morgan was inspired by some ribald conversation to apply for the Welsh franchise. He contacted by phone another Welshman, Wynford Vaughan-Thomas, and together they decided to invite the most popular Welsh Establishment figure in the land, Lord Harlech, former British Ambassador to the United States, to head their group. To their amazement and delight, he agreed. The next move was to recruit an array of Welsh and West Country businessmen and financial interests to provide the £2,450,000 capital required to enable any contender to join the hunt-the-franchise game. The capital would be used either to build new studios or take over the existing studios of the incumbent company, TWW. There was no shortage of investors.

Finally there were the glamour names of the entertainment world with which it was hoped to dazzle the not particularly worldly group of ITA Governors whom they had to impress. With such talent, ran the Welsh group's argument, programmes could be made by a regional company that could be exported abroad and thus contribute to Britain's unhealthy balance of payments. To further such a selfless national purpose, the newly named Harlech TV had recruited to their colours such sparkling personalities as actors Richard Burton, Elizabeth Taylor, and Stanley Baker, opera singer Geraint Evans, and comedian Harry Secombe. Said Secombe of this array of Welsh talent: 'If they don't get the contract, they can always form a glee club.'³

The company applying for the London weekend franchise was also stuffed with star names. There was that man for all occasions and all programmes, David Frost, supported by the Conservative MP and TV commentator, Aidan Crawley, Chairman of the Group. The most formidable personality in their application was John Freeman, who at the time was British High Commissioner in India and a former editor of the influential left-wing journal, the *New Statesman*. As a very successful TV performer in a series of impressive interviews called *Face to Face*, Freeman combined the credentials of a knowledgeable communications man with the prestige of a distinguished diplomatic figure. It was a flight to India by David Frost that succeeded in getting Mr Freeman to act as Deputy Chairman of the Group, with the possibility that he would become the Company's full-time Head of Current Affairs when he left the Government service sometime in the early summer of 1968. What was *not* revealed in London Weekend's application or in the interview with the selection board was that at the very time Freeman agreed to join the consortium, he knew that he might be offered the ambassadorial post in Washington and that if it were offered to him, he would accept it.

Supplementing the obvious attractions of Frost, Freeman, and Crawley, the London Weekend group had also managed to lure into their corporeal net some of the most experienced and dynamic executives in British TV. From the BBC, they had acquired Michael Peacock, Programme Head of BBC-1 and the man with direct responsibility for the programmes of the largest broadcasting organization in the world. Peacock was

to be the company's Managing Director. From Rediffusion TV
came that Company's Programme Controller, Cyril Bennett,
to take over much the same job for the new group. Other
impressive figures who had agreed to switch their allegiance
from the BBC were Doreen Stephens, head of the Corporation's
children's programmes; Frank Muir, who had supervised
comedy shows for the BBC; and Humphrey Burton, who had
been responsible for the BBC's music and opera output. There
was also Clive Irving, a well-known journalist and media
expert.

In spite of these delectable nosegays of talent, attractively
selected and arranged to appeal to the most discriminating
selection committee, the general view in newspaper and TV
circles was that they had little chance of tempting the ITA to
make any radical change in the existing set-up.

A leader in *The Guardian* was forthright about the minimal
possibilities of a new company edging out an existing company.

'Whatever it says in the Act, a newcomer's chance of getting
a television broadcasting franchise is about one in 50. The
ITA has made room for one more contractor, but that is the
limit. The 13 established ones can be challenged because the
law says so. Whether they can be displaced is another matter.
The ITA might arrange a marriage or two but—like the
Forsytes—the family will stick together.'[4]

The most obvious reason for the assumption that there
would be no change was that to disenfranchise any of the sitting
companies would be a tacit admission that Lord Hill and his
Authority had seriously failed in one of their most important
responsibilities. After all, the Authority had for a number of
years sat in on all network planning-committee meetings.
Its officials had scrupulously studied the schedules of the
companies, and even the scripts of the programmes, and were
in a position to veto anything they did not like. Its representatives were in constant touch with every company and were
aware of the balance of their output and the quality of the
people running them. It was, therefore, logical for the existing
contractors to assume that what they had been doing was being
done with the full support of the ITA. At the very least, if
their performance had been in any way wanting, wouldn't the
Authority have given them some warning or notice of its displeasure? No such hint of disapproval had been communicated
to any of the fourteen companies when Lord Hill advertised
for applicants to displace them.

But what about the plight of the shareholders in any company that suddenly lost its franchise? Could they, or should they, be deprived of their major financial asset, and what effect would such a decision have on the investment attractions of independent TV in the future? Would it not encourage companies to make a profit as quickly as they could, with little regard to programme standards, if they were always conscious of the fragility of their status and the potential shortness of their stay? What about the stability of the industry? Would the uncertainty act as a deterrent to any meaningful long-term planning?

In spite of the fact that most informed opinion viewed the whole selection procedure as little more than bureaucratic window-dressing, both the existing and aspiring companies duly faced the thirteen Governors of the ITA in a series of hush-hush interviews.

John Grigg in *The Guardian* voiced some misgivings about the way in which these new franchises were being handed out:

'It is odd that parliament should hive off such a big responsibility—with such an important bearing on the democratic process itself—to a small body of people appointed by the Postmaster General. If the selecting body were a group of MPs, holding open hearings in the different areas—with submission and questioning of applicants on the record—justice might more actually be done, and would anyway more obviously be seen to be done.

'Lord Hill and his colleagues can be relied on to do their very best, without fear or favour, but whom do they represent? They have no title to represent the British people, on whose behalf they are acting in a matter of serious consequence. They are not responsible to Parliament. They have no special expertise in judging either the financial or the technical and artistic credentials of the applicants. They are just a random body of nominees. . . .

'The relations between commercial TV and the press, the taxation of ITV companies and the structure of control, need to be looked at afresh. The present setup is neither a garden nor a jungle; it is more like a rubbish heap.'[5]

The authoritative journal, *The Economist*, also showed some of this concern.

A uniquely curious event is unfolding in British public life. A statutory body is in the process of deciding which 15 limited companies should be granted the monopoly right for six years to share a total annual income now running at over £80 million which should (more or less) produce total annual pre-tax profits of something over £15 million. More-over, this largesse will be distributed, or withheld, largely on the basis of past public performance.

And yet this statutory body is being allowed to reach its decisions without any serious public discussion whatsoever. Hardly a word of fact, analysis or opinion appears in print. It is as if there was a conspiracy of silence in the whole British press.[6]

Finally on 11 June 1967, at the ITA's offices in the Brompton Road, Lord Hill announced to the press the decisions about the new franchises. In keeping with his concern about the effect the news would have on the shares of the dispossessed companies, the announcement was made on a Sunday when the Stock Exchange was closed. Presumably, this would give the unfor-tunate losers some hours to take defensive measures to cushion the impact of the news on their share prices.

First, the losers. One major company—Rediffusion—was to lose its franchise and to be merged as a minority partner with ABC TV to run the five weekdays in London. One regional company—TWW in Wales—was to lose its franchise. Another regional company—Scottish TV—was to have its fiscal struc-ture altered so that the Thomson Organization—whose most significant contribution to TV was Lord Thomson's phrase 'a licence to print money'—would now be only a minority share-holder.

Next, the winners. The Harlech consortium—now known as Harlech TV—was to take over TWW's franchise in Wales. The Telefusion Yorkshire consortium—now known as York-shire TV—was given the Yorkshire contract on the under-standing that certain newspapers, co-operative societies, trade unions, and entertainment firms in rival consortia would be allowed some financial participation.[7] The London consortium —now known as London Weekend TV—with its roster of glamour TV and journalist names was given the capital city's weekend franchise. Again it was understood that *The Observer*, the *Daily Telegraph*, and *The Economist*—which were associated with unsuccessful bidders—should be given an opportunity to invest in the new weekend company.

Justifying these changes, Lord Hill said that the Authority was guided by two main principles.

First, and all the time, we have borne in mind the quality of the programme service which Independent Television will offer in the new contract period. We have scrutinized the applications from this point of view because the Authority can have no more important consideration in awarding contracts.

The second principle may be put in the form of an answer to a question. Must the doors of Independent Television remain forever closed to new applicants, however good they are? If the answer is 'Yes,' then those companies already appointed are there for all time. But the Authority's answer must, of course, be 'No.'

It follows that the choice may well be not between a good applicant and a bad applicant, but between a *good* applicant and one which, after full consideration, the Authority believes will be a better one.

Although the war between Israel and Egypt was then at its height, Lord Hill's TV bombshell managed the next morning to explode as the lead front-page story in eight out of ten national newspapers.

'LORD HILL NAMES WINNERS IN CONTRACTS BATTLE: FROST JOINS TYCOONS IN ITV SHAKE-UP' was the *Daily Mirror* headline, and it reflected the general surprise.[8]

On the whole, Fleet Street, although taken aback by the changes, was pleased by Lord Hill's new look for commercial TV. Said Peter Black of the *Daily Mail* about the disenfranchised companies: 'They bored the ITA until a change became a shrieking imperative.' Said James Thomas in the *Daily Express*: 'No television producing company can ever again get the idea that once it gets what Lord Thomson called "a licence to print money" it is automatically there for life. . . . The Authority is at last ready to put new zest, vitality and ideas into a programme service which stands accused of hypnotizing its public with unadventurous monotony.'

The crucial issue, however, was whether Lord Hill's changes were for the better. Would the injection of this new element into the ITV alliance really change or vitalize much? What could these three new companies do to bring a fresh stimulus and excitement to the sluggish sameness of commercial television's ratings-conscious output? Would the shock of Lord Hill's action shake the old companies into striving—even if only to avoid their colleagues' fate in six years' time—for something different, more mature, more imaginative? As time was to prove, nothing much would change.

Once the winners had been announced, the slide-rules came

out and the City began rubbing its hands in anticipation of the spoils. It was calculated that both London Weekend Television and Yorkshire Television would be making profits in the region of £1,500,000 in their first years, and that Harlech Television could make anything from £300,000 to £100,000 in the same time. It was variously predicted that the shares of London Weekend would appreciate by mid-June 1968 anywhere from 276% to 650%. Yorkshire's appreciation, because it had costly new studios to build, was expected to be more modest—between 60% and 156%. Harlech's expectation of sudden wealth was calculated to be anywhere between 100% and 559%.[9]

During the year in which the new companies were preparing themselves for action, speculation about the worth of the new companies reached ecstatic heights. Financial experts, gazing at the great future, could see only rich pickings for those lucky enough to have caught Lord Hill's beneficent eye.

Shareholders in a very short time could have made capital gains ranging between 300% and 500%. For some shareholders who only paid a shilling a share and sold out quickly, the capital gains amounted to no less than 1,650%.

But as it eventually turned out, the shareholders who sold out before the companies ever went on the air were the fortunate ones. As we shall see, unforeseen circumstances severly curtailed the expected profits. The fact, however, remains that all informed financial opinion at that time was agreed upon the potential riches lying in the wake of these franchises. The ITA never contradicted these bonanza forecasts and it must, therefore, be assumed that it had few qualms or objections to such riches being made through its bounty. If, in the event, profits turned out to be less than anticipated, it was not the Authority's doing. Its responsibility ended with the selection of the companies. If some of the companies were in television purely to make a quick financial killing in six years, there is no evidence that such a prospect unduly perturbed the ITA.

Surely it would have been right and proper for Lord Hill to lay down certain criteria for a return on capital and a reasonable profit rate. This might have gone some way in deterring the get-rich-quick merchants from prospecting in the telly gold mine, might have ensured that only those who were genuinely interested in the challenge and stimulation of producing television programmes would bother to apply for franchises.

Yet, despite the graceless rush and the profit speculation which characterized the pursuit of the franchises, when the new companies took to the air in mid-1968, the public looked forward to a new kind of TV. The prospect of something different and exciting on the commercial network had been whipped up to a mild frenzy by the publicity handouts and by an optimistic press.

Disillusion set in fast. Like a parade of electronic beauty queens, each company, accompanied by a fanfare of publicity, displayed its most obvious wares in a series of openings in the summer of 1968. These premieres, alas, were a presage of things to come. Harlech Television turned up with a first night that resembled in spirit a mayoralty dinner at the Palladium, not made any more appetizing by a number of technical faults that blacked-out part of the transmission. Yorkshire, Thames Television, and London Weekend had their introductory first nights bedevilled by a technicians' strike which not only dimmed their lustre but cost in the first week something like £300,000 of anticipated revenue.

After that, disasters fell thick and fast on commercial television, and particularly on the new companies. Taking advantage of the two-week technicians' strike, the BBC aggressively filled its schedules with popular light entertainment like the *Val Doonican Show*, *Marty*, westerns, and the most simian programme on the air, *It's A Knockout*.

The ratings, although there was some doubt about their reliability in the early weeks because a new company—JICTAR[10]—was using new methods to measure audience sizes, showed a serious fall of viewers. By some calculations, 4,000,000 viewers had deserted the commercial network.

Ever conscious of the cost per thousand viewers, the advertisers began to exert indirect pressure on the companies to retrieve its lost audience. There was much talk of a cut in television advertising appropriations by the agencies and hints that some advertisers were about to switch their revenue to newspapers and magazines. Executives of some advertising agencies deplored the absence of programmes like *Double Your Money* and *Take Your Pick*—popular and moronic quiz games that had made top ratings for twelve years—and hoped that they would soon be back on the air. 'A catastrophic situation,' one advertising man was reported as saying. Said another: 'The present state of things cannot continue beyond two or three months.'

It was quite clear that no one interpreted the dissatisfaction of the advertisers as a call for better quality television, more serious drama, more committed or responsible current affairs programmes. The reaction of most of the companies to their falling ratings was to return to less demanding, more familiar, and more orthodox entertainment.

Weary disappointment was expressed by all the important British television critics. The *Daily Mail*'s Peter Black reported after a month's viewing: 'So far there's pathetically little evidence that the new era of ITV is going to do any better than the old.' Maurice Wiggin of *The Sunday Times*, contemplating the same period, wrote, 'I may be less critical of the new era than some of my colleagues, for the simple reason that I expected less . . . all the names and most of the faces behind the new schedules were quite, quite old. So why expect a revolution?'

As if a bad press and low ratings weren't burdens enough for the new companies, they were hit by a series of financial blows as well. The technicians' strike lost them substantial revenue; the capital costs of converting to colour were more than expected; a minor recession hit the land with a subsequent reduction in advertising budgets; Yorkshire TV lost £250,000 in advertising revenue when its giant transmitting mast on Ealy Moor collapsed in a gale; and finally, the least expected blow of all—the Labour Chancellor, in his budget of April 1969, increased the total advertising levy on all companies by some £3,000,000. This additional, surprise tax was particularly hard on the new companies who had no large past profits to cushion them.

'The rates introduced in 1964 have remained unaltered,' said the Chancellor, Roy Jenkins, in his budget speech, justifying this latest squeeze on commercial TV's income. 'The ITA has estimated that profits before tax in the past three years averaged well over 40% on capital employed, and in my view the community should have a bigger share in the value of these publicly created concessions.'*

Sir Lew Grade, Managing Director of ATV, shared the industry's reaction to the Chancellor's latest impost. 'It's horrible,' he cried, 'I can't say anything more.'

Thus in a few short weeks all the high promise of a revitalized, stimulating commercial network had collapsed. Lord Hill, the man chiefly responsible for the new set-up, was no longer around

---

* The new rates which came into force in July 1969 were nil on the first £500,000 of gross advertising receipts; 7% on the next £1,000,000; 25% on the next 2,500,000; 35% on the next £6,000,000 and 47½% on the remainder. The previous rates had been: nil on the first £1,500,000; 25% on the next £6,000,000; and 45% on anything over £7,500,000.

to be blamed for these sorry developments. A grateful Prime Minister—presumably impressed by his handling of these matters—had wafted him off to more significant activities as the head of the BBC. As Hill's successor, it was Lord Aylestone's thankless job to find explanations and excuses for the humiliations yet to come.

There is little doubt that London Weekend TV was the company which epitomized most the progressive shift in commercial TV's thinking. Located in the nation's capital, LWTV had easy access to most of the talent—cultural, artistic, political, scientific, educational—in the land. It was brimming over with some of the brightest TV executives and creative men in the business, and was the one company in the entire network that appeared to have been enfranchised more for the strength of its programming potential than for the financial reliability and respectability of its backers.

Its articulate and vigorous Managing Director, Michael Peacock, had made it almost an article of faith that London Weekend would be more adventurous and more mature in its programming than the previous holder of the franchise, Sir Lew Grade's ATV. 'The trouble is that ITV believes that people stop thinking at weekends,' Peacock had said when he went over to commercial TV from the BBC.[11]

Then late in April 1969 came the news that London Weekend had closed down its Public Affairs Department. This was considered a major defeat for the company since it was always assumed that London Weekend would be making a special contribution in the field of current affairs, in documentaries and news features. Thirteen people were sacked.

The final surrender to the inevitable—and the ultimate fadeout of the few remaining hopes of better television—came when Cyril Bennett, London Weekend's Programme Controller, released his plans for the autumn and winter of 1969–70.

'ITV RETURNS TO THE OLD FAVOURITES' ran a newspaper headline over the story in which Bennett announced a schedule of family comedy, variety programmes, and old films. 'The first duty of a commercial station is to survive,' said Mr Bennett, justifying the company's abandonment of its altruistic aspirations. 'What do you think the public regard television as—a teaching medium?'

It was bad luck for London Weekend that this announcement of its future plans should coincide early in July 1969 with the publication of a pamphlet issued by the Free Communications Group—a ginger group of journalists and broadcasting men demanding a larger control of the media in which they work. This pamphlet, called *The Open Secret*, contained the confidential document produced by Aidan Crawley and David Frost when they applied to the ITA for the London franchise. The yawning chasm between the statements made in this embarrassing document and the record of London Weekend's programme performance after almost a year was now revealed in all its shabbiness. This revelation merely intensified the suspicion that somewhere along the line a confidence trick had been played upon the nation.

Under the headline 'The Scandal of London Weekend,' I wrote in the *Evening Standard* on 9 July 1969:

Compared to what London Weekend has actually done, the programme vistas projected by this document read as if they were written by someone with the imagination of a Jules Verne.

Goodies are piled upon goodies. A Current Affairs Unit—already disbanded—was to provide a 45-minute news programme every Sunday afternoon; a 30-minute examination of controversies every Friday or Sunday evening; six to seven major historical and social documentaries a year.

In addition, there were to be a number of science series called The Inventors, The New Bedlam, Do Animals Speak?, Nobel Prizewinners, The Formative Years. On top of that there would be another 45 minutes every Sunday of cultural programmes. The company would be a 'major originator of television drama.' Occasionally an entire evening would be devoted to a single cultural event.

As if this were not Elysium enough, there would be a wide range of comedy and variety shows, children's and religious programmes, adult education, regional and leisure programmes. All in two and a half days a week, excluding mornings!

What it has been reduced to can be seen by comparing in detail what ATV was showing at peak time in the first week in July 1968 and what London Weekend offered in the first week of July 1969.

London Weekend is distinguished only by the fact that its films are older than ATV's, that its comedy and variety shows are worse than ATV's.

In outlining their plans for the autumn, Cyril Bennett, London Weekend's Programme Controller, suggested no shame nor embarrassment nor contrition in promising a return to all the old, stale ideas his company had vowed to eliminate.

In a statement that might become as notorious as Lord Thomson's remark about 'a licence to print money,' he declared that 'the first duty of a commercial television station is to survive!'

Is it? I would have thought that its first duty was service to the public, a maintenance of television standards, a moral obligation to stand by the promises that gave it a franchise.

If it has discovered that it cannot achieve the standards that it promised to a public authority—and indirectly to the people—then its first duty is suicide or a gracious withdrawal to make room for others who will attempt more energetically and efficiently to achieve a level of broadcasting that the ITA presumably considered desirable.

Once the ITA's badly conceived policy of secrecy was discredited by the revelation of London Weekend's application, the press took up with relish the whole question of the allotment of these new franchises. Soon the applications of all the new companies, instead of blushing unseen in ITA's files, were unveiled in the papers in all their persuasive optimism. In its Insight column on the main feature page, *The Sunday Times* summarized the contents of all these winning applications and concluded that they were all devised 'for magnifying a desired image, rather than a vehicle for the transmission of information. All three are minor classics for public relations technique.'[12]

Harlech Television's application was written in a style becoming the lyricism and loquacity of Wales. The broadcaster Wynford Vaughan-Thomas, who was one of the main authors of this eloquent prospectus, recalled with relish the circumstances under which it was written. 'I can tell you, that application wasn't written on beer,' he said. 'I decanted some rare vintages. I remember at one point I decanted my last bottle of Lafitte '45.'[13]

Its plans for programmes included a series of confrontations with distinguished and humble figures in every walk of life; a weekly survey of art exhibitions called 'Round the Galleries'; some programmes featuring Harry Secombe; and a group of shows grandiloquently bracketed under the title 'International Star Programme.' These included three films in which Richard Burton would discuss the actor's art, give his recollections of the mining valley in which he grew up, and host a rollicking epic showing 'the drama, tension, laughter and triumph of a Welsh international rugby match against England.' Another International Star Programme was to be an interview with Elizabeth Taylor by John Morgan. Stanley Baker and Geraint Evans had also promised to contribute programmes in this series. After a year of transmission, Harlech Television had delivered, of this cornucopia of promises, only a documentary with Geraint Evans and one programme starring Stanley Baker.

Whether the new companies had lived up to their promises in detail would not, of course, matter very much if they had in essence fulfilled the spirit of their applications. Presumably they had been chosen to bring in a new mood, a different excitement to the commercial channel which had grown stale and rigid in its ideas and planning. By their dynamism and competitive ingenuity, it must have been expected that they would force the other companies to respond by throwing away musty formula and adapt, as one of their commercials might put it, a tingling freshness. Were any of these hopes realized?

Under the heading 'ITV BACK TO WHERE IT WAS A YEAR AGO' the leader column of the periodical *Television Today* said, 'The return of *Take Your Pick* this autumn underlines, if any more emphasis were needed, what is now obvious about independent television: it is incapable of real improvement. Whatever claim the big five companies made that they would give a new deal to ITA have now no value: things are very much as before the new contracts were awarded. There have been new programmes of all kinds, as so there would have been had the old contracts all been renewed, but the overall impact of programming is much the same—safe, boring and predictable. . . .'[14]

Julian Critchley, *The Times*'s television critic, summed up his impression of London Weekend's record with these words: 'London Weekend has suffered from too wide a gap between promise and performance. Judged by what we were led to expect, results have been lamentable. What has gone unnoticed is the fact that it is by no means the worst offender. Thames Television had no prospectus for anyone to pinch: it made no promises, and in consequence what it has done has gone unnoticed.'[15]

Although most of the television contractors discreetly decided that a dignified silence was the only stance to take in the face of this hurricane of bad publicity, Michael Peacock of London Weekend, made a courageous effort to justify the record of his company.

In an interview given to James Thomas of the *Daily Express*, he bared his breast about his company.

> We have made 101 mistakes. We were all very naïve. We thought it would be an interesting challenge to change the pattern of television from what we believed was a dreary and played-out schedule. But now I kick myself for having been party to stocking up expectations about change. We certainly did not appreciate the problems involved in getting the public to take to new ideas.
>
> We, at London Weekend started out to make changes too quickly. The interesting challenge turned out to be a strait-jacket. . . . We have got to a point where no one can take risks. Why should we spend £500,000 on a serial which may fail when for peanuts we can buy a quiz from another company. . . . A programme that gives you money in the bank is better than one which gives you a headache.[16]

Unperturbed by all the fuss, impatient with any questioning of its decisions, smug in its remote omniscience, was the Independent Television Authority. It, at least, had no visible regrets about what it had done. Said Sir Robert Fraser, ITA's Director General and its *eminence grise* since the inception of commercial television:

> After fifteen years of appointing companies, the ITA was perfectly capable of making its own realistic estimate of what in fact the performance of a company was likely to be.
>
> Having made its relative assessments, its duty was to appoint the applicant judged best of those available, and then ensure that its performance came up to the standards required by the Television Act and by the Authority itself.
>
> In that context, catching companies out by discovering that they had not fulfilled this or that intention is at best childish, at worst a bore.[17]

That astute and witty observer of the contemporary scene, Bernard Levin, immediately recognized the farcical potentialities of Sir Robert's ill-chosen remarks. In his column in the *Daily Mail* he wrote:

> There have been further sensational developments at Dustbin House, headquarters of Trash Television. It will be remembered that the present consortium in charge of the station got the franchise to transmit programmes seven days

a week throughout the country by announcing that in the first six months of their operation they would screen hour-long interviews with the Pope, Mr Dubček, Bertrand Russell, The Dalai Lama, Bob Dylan, Elizabeth Taylor, the Kray Brothers and Martin Bormann, and would also show programmes including the Bolshoi Ballet, the proceedings of the British Association, a heart transplant operation, a meeting of the Soviet Politburo, and fifty new songs by the Beatles.

When, after a year, the company had put out nothing but repeats of an old *I Love Lucy* series, Sir Hamish Mice, the Secretary of the Television Board, was asked for his comments and replied: 'Catching companies out by discovering that they had not fulfilled this or that intention is at best childish, at worst a bore.'[18]

On the morning of 19 September 1969 every national newspaper in Britain led its front page with the news that Michael Peacock, the forty-year-old Managing Director of London Weekend, had been sacked.

After ten days of discussion and argument between management and staff over Peacock's dismissal, six key executives of London Weekend Television handed in their resignations.[19]

Said Frank Muir, one of those who left: 'The real thing is that the company now is not the company I joined. What we disagreed about was the change in top management.

'Lots of reasons have been given for Michael Peacock's sacking. But none of them have been convincing. It's an important question of principle. It's not about culture versus commerce. It's about ethos and atmosphere.'[20]

With the departure of Peacock and his six executives there was little left but the shell of the company that had offered itself to the ITA for the London franchise. A few months later Cyril Bennett, the Programme Controller, and Tito Burns, head of the company's variety programmes, also departed. The ITA was now faced with the fact that not only had the promises of London Weekend disintegrated into little more than hollow laughter but that the shape and essence of the organization had changed so fundamentally that the original company virtually ceased to exist.

At the height of the fuss about the broken promises, the Authority stubbornly maintained that it was the men that counted and not their original proposals. Yet in the case of London Weekend both the promises *and* the men were now gone in just a year. Of the ten experienced programme names that the company had used to bedazzle the Authority in its application, only four remained—Aidan Crawley, David Frost (who was spending about half his time in America), Tom Margerison, and Clive Irving. John Freeman, Michael Peacock, Cyril Bennett, Humphrey Burton, Frank Muir, and Doreen Stephens had left—or, in the case of Freeman, never turned up.

What then was the ITA, under Lord Aylestone, going to do about it? Nothing. What was the Postmaster General, John Stonehouse, going to do about it? Nothing.

'WEEKEND TELEMESS' was how a headline over an *Evening Standard* leader summarized the situation. 'The real guilty party is, of course, the Independent Television Authority,' it said. 'No exercise of public regulation since the war has been as incompetent or naïve as the procedure by which franchises for commercial television stations have been secretly awarded.'[21]

There was one important figure, however, who did not share the concern of independent observers about the baffled incompetence, declining standards, and dull resignation shown by the recent events in commercial television. He was Lord Aylestone, Chairman of the ITA.

In a long interview given to the advertising and press magazine *Campaign*, Lord Aylestone showed complacency and insensitivity about the shape of Independent Television. Asked what steps he had taken about the exodus of executives from London Weekend, he replied, 'We have taken no step or action whatsoever, other than see the Management. . . . Our action in this particular problem could only start if and when—I repeat if and when—we feel that programme standards are falling.'

'But,' protested one of his interviewers, 'there has been a lot of criticism about the quality of ITV programmes generally.'

'I find it a little difficult to understand criticisms of programme content,' replied Lord Aylestone, in a classical statement of bland philistinism, 'when currently we are getting 17 programmes out of the Top Twenty almost every week. Our audience shares are 54's and 55's in competition not with one BBC channel, but with two.'[22]

It is to be expected that the commercial entrepreneurs who run the television companies should convince themselves that high ratings indicate quality. But that the man who has been set over them to act as a guardian of standards and an influence for better television should be equating excellence with popularity like the most zealous advertising man, is a disturbing insight into the programming philosophy that pervades the Independent Television Authority.

While the troubles of London Weekend were making high-pitched noises on the front pages of Britain's newspapers, on the financial pages the news of commercial television sounded a more sombre, insistent note. The theme of this threnody was 'We are not making enough money, give us more.' In turn each company reported substantially lower profits out of television in 1969 and for the same reasons—decreased advertising revenue, increased costs, higher capital expenditure because of colour, the presence of a fifth large company, and the Government levy.

Although the market as a whole had been a falling one, television shares plummeted well below the average index, declining to anywhere from 50% to 75% of their previous values.

Lord Shawcross, Chairman of Thames Television, in his annual report, ruefully protested, 'In the early days of independent television large profits were made. They no longer are, but . . . the idea that independent television is a gold mine dies hard.'[23]

The basic financial argument being put up loudly and in concert by the companies was that they were being milked so vigorously by the levy and taxes that the quality of their programmes would seriously suffer. Considering the kind of programmes being put out by commercial television when it was rolling in money, one might well wonder to what ultimate depths the contractors envisaged their product falling.

The return on capital was calculated to be only 10%, which according to Lord Shawcross, 'is utterly inadequate to attract capital into this important industry; companies have to make the most drastic cuts in expenditure.'[24]

It was, indeed, nothing like the return got in the good old days before the levy, and much lower than the £19 million made in 1967–68 when the return on capital was about 40%, or the £10 million in 1968–69 when the return was something like 25% on capital employed. And since most companies had always been in the habit of distributing the bulk of their post-tax profits to shareholders, even a 10% return to shareholders in the so-called disaster year of 1969–70 would still have been a larger gain—to contradict a statement by Lord Aylestone—than could be had from most building societies.

It might also be noted that Lord Shawcross's concern about the difficulties of 'attracting capital into this important industry' is hardly convincing in the light of ITV's long practice of pumping capital out of television almost as fast as it came in. The diversification activities of the companies—over £80,000,000 had been shifted into non-television activities during their history—have always been a sad indication of the indifference of some of these companies to the long-term interests of the medium. Indeed, at the very time ITV was publicly wringing its hands about the paucity of money available for programmes, cash was being siphoned into activities like music publishing and night clubs, precisely in order to cushion shareholders against bleak times in television.

There were, indeed, some stony-hearted citizens who refused to be moved by the wails of anguish emanating from the telly tycoons. Labour MP Christopher Mayhew, for example, who had been a vigorous and consistent critic of commercial TV ever since its inception, reflected the scepticism of many in his letter to *The Times*.

> At the risk of seeming uncharitable (and it is a hard, cold winter), I recommend that we taxpayers reject the piteous appeal for financial assistance being made to us by Sir Lew Grade, Lord Shawcross and other Independent Television shareholders. . . .
>
> Nobody likes to see these unfortunate people suffer, and the value of their shares has certainly declined sharply. But before we add their claims for relief to those of the teachers, nurses, old age pensioners, holders of War Loan, and taxpayers in general, we should be told:
>
> (1) What happened to the vast profits made by shareholders in the past? How far are they being made available to help the companies through the leaner times ahead? . . .
>
> Sir Lew's begging bowl is merely one symptom of a growing malaise afflicting the ITV. Other symptoms have been the scandal of the Harlech and London Weekend prospectuses, the continuing servility of the Authority towards the companies and the exodus of the professional broadcasters.
>
> Parliament should give no financial relief to ITV shareholders without a searching examination of ITV as a whole, followed by drastic reforms. . . .[25]

The companies, however, were not to be denied. They had had much experience exerting pressure on Governments for what they wanted and they put their formidable techniques into action once again to get the Labour Government to ease their financial burdens.

It did not escape the attention of some observers that the campaign being mounted with such efficiency by the commercial television interests had a certain familiar quality about it. Wrote Bernard Levin in the *Daily Mail*:

> Every argument, every method of persuasion, every action of the commercial television lobby is an exact replica of the campaign waged in the same interest in 1963. The careful leaks to the Press of tendentious figures; the activities of the MPs of the commercial television lobby; the threats that standards would be lowered; the claim that the impost could not be recovered from advertisers; everything down to the last detail of what Mr Stonehouse is now experiencing is to be found [in *The Greasy Pole*, the autobiography of Reginald Bevins, the Conservative Postmaster General who introduced the first television levy]. . . . I hope Mr Stonehouse will take a leaf out of his predecessor's book, and greet the cries of wolf with his thumb to his nose.[26]

But Mr Stonehouse did not adopt such a forthright and vulgar posture. The campaign worked. On 16 March 1970 the Postmaster General announced measures which would reduce the total levy to all the companies by about £6,000,000. He also informed the Commons that the finances of all the companies were being referred to the Prices and Incomes Board for an independent assessment of their financial operation. Thus the £3,000,000 which the Chancellor had taken from the Contractors in 1969 budget had been restored in less than a year, and another £3,000,000 had been handed back to them as well.

'It was an astounding decision,' said Christopher Mayhew, when the matter was debated in the Commons on 23 March 1970. 'The Minister said he was merely relieving them of an imposition, but it was a hand-out to the most prosperous, most influential and least deserving lobby in the country.'

But Mr Mayhew's protest represented very much a minority view in the House of Commons.

If, however, the Government thought that the handing over of £6,000,000 to the companies was going to quiet their grievances, it was quickly to be disillusioned. The complaining and groaning went on as shrilly and persistently as ever. This time it was directed towards, not a reduction of the levy, but its elimination altogether. With the election of a Conservative

Government in June 1970, and the appointment of a Tory Postmaster General, or Minister of Posts and Telecommunications as he was now called,[27] in the person of Christopher Chataway, the predictions of disaster by television tycoons became more insistent and hysterical than ever.

It was during this nadir in the fortunes of commercial television—humiliation over the new franchises, the fiasco at London Weekend, the weakened financial position—that the ITA early in 1970 advertised for a new Director General. Sir Robert Fraser, the man who had held the post since the very inception of the ITA in 1954, was retiring in September at the age of sixty-six. Born and educated in Australia, a former leader-writer on the Labour newspaper, the *Daily Herald,* and the Director General of the Government's Central Office of Information from 1946 to 1954, Fraser was undoubtedly the guiding spirit and mentor of commercial television. Through the reigns of four chairmen of the ITA—Clark, Kirkpatrick, Hill, and Aylestone—one can detect the consistent style and influence of Sir Robert. Under his aegis the ITA maintained a protective, paternal relation to the companies, justifying their profits, supporting their fiscal battles, commending their record, applauding their programme policies. Rarely did it act as an impartial guardian of the public interest, willing to chastise its charges or supervise their actions.

Sir Robert's conception of commercial television as 'people's television' opposed the relatively elitist approach of the BBC. For him it was primarily a medium for entertainment, whose success could be gauged through the people's approval as recorded in the television ratings. He was a firm and vigorous advocate of the regional principle which undoubtedly prevented the commercial channel from being London-bound and London-dominated and which enabled companies like Granada to make a distinctive and local contribution to the nation's broadcasting. He must also be given a great deal of credit for his championing of a less stuffy and less confined approach to the transmission of news and for his encouraging ITN reporters not to rely on information gathered by newspapers and agencies, but to go out and get their own stories.

Under Sir Robert Fraser commercial television certainly established itself as the most popular TV service in the land. It was also the service best liked by politicians because it was more amenable to their demands and less stubborn than the BBC in insisting on its independence. It also made a large number of shareholders very rich and very comfortable indeed.

Thus as the architect of independent television, Sir Robert had built a solid, opulent, and vulgar mansion. But when he left, the edifice was already showing signs that its foundations were beginning to crumble. The new companies had not stopped the decline in programme standards. The old companies—short of money partly because of their diversification activities which Sir Robert had not openly discouraged—served up the same programme mixture as before and justified themselves by pointing to the restricting tolls of the levy.

Even Sir Robert's policy of regionalism was beginning to look very shaky by the time he departed. The geographical overlapping of some of the areas made mergers between the smaller companies attractive, even essential, if they were to remain economically viable. In August 1970 Yorkshire Television and Tyne Tees Television—although maintaining their individual identities—formed a joint holding company, combining their operating resources. This was the first crack in Sir Robert's rigid regional conception. Lord Harlech's plea for a reduction in the total number of companies contributed to the likelihood that a different way of serving regional needs would have to be found when the present contracts run out in 1976.

Thus the electronic house that Sir Robert had built was visibly disintegrating. Its major social purpose—to provide competition for the BBC—had been accomplished. But only the most partisan of commercial television advocates could honestly state that the BBC had been improved by such competition. The evidence clearly showed that competition had lowered BBC's awareness of its sense of public duty and that broadcasting standards, on the whole, had deteriorated.

With so many difficult problems to be faced and with its reputation in the public eye at an all-time low, it was assumed that the Independent Television Authority would select for Sir Robert's successor a man not only conversant with the intricate ways of the medium, but one whose background and experience would enable him to face on equal terms the wily company executives and the knowledgeable civil servants of the Post Office with whom he would have to plan and negotiate the future of ITV.

With its unerring instinct for a course of action that was bound to delight its critics and dismay its friends, the ITA astonished everyone but itself by announcing that Brian Young would be its new Director General. Who? Brian Young. No one in the television world had ever heard of him. The surprise was inevitable because in its advertisement for the job, the

Authority had explicitly emphasized that it was looking for someone 'already prominent in television.'

As a former headmaster of Charterhouse public school and a Director of the Nuffield Foundation for six years, what could he possibly know about television? 'Nothing very much' admitted the forty-seven-year-old Mr Young. But he was hoping to read up about it!

The press was simply baffled. Not since the Emperor Caligula had made his horse a Consul, said some, had there been such an astonishing appointment. The pressure groups—the 76 Group and the Free Communications Group—who had been insisting that the new Director General come from within the industry, were reduced to almost incoherent splutters. Alan Sapper, Secretary of the ACTT, the television technicians' and directors' union, said, 'We consider the way the appointment was made and the actual person appointed was outrageous owing to his admitted lack of knowledge and experience in the television medium. . . . Mr Young has said he has had a colour television set for a year. I have had a size 5 football for about two years, but that doesn't make me George Best.'[28]

Echoing this scepticism was Kenneth Adam, the former controller of Television at the BBC, writing in the *Evening News*.

What chance has Brian Young when he meets Sir Lew Grade, Lord Bernstein, Howard Thomas and the other masterful entrepreneurs of the programme companies—and make no mistake they are masters of their craft—of asserting his authority over them. *Because that must happen if ITV is to improve its standards.* [My italics.]

Authority is the essential quality in a Director General. He is the ITA, if he is the right man and choses to be, just as Greene was the BBC and Curran is not.

Eton and Cheltenham, a first class in classics and a half-blue for fives, composing chess problems and playing the clarinet—these may be the background to a good and rounded life, but they do not equip anyone for the power game, to enter the lists against the bold bad barons of high finance and low showbiz.[29]

The new Director General did not have to wait long before he was plunged into one of those awkward crises that have haunted commercial television since its inception. The situation in London Weekend had continued to deteriorate with low profits, low morale, and low prospects. But when Rupert Murdoch, an Australian newspaper proprietor, took over effective control of London Weekend by purchasing 8.25 % of the equity, Brian Young revealed a firm resistance to this development that surprised many of his detractors. Murdoch's success with British papers like the *News of the World* and the *Sun*, which thrived on nude pictures and sensationalism, and his Australian television station whose programmes were largely composed of old films and American series, hardly gave him the sort of image considered suitable for the head of one of the most important television companies in Britain. Young made it quite clear to the London Weekend board that if Murdoch were to dominate the company, the ITA might consider that the nature of the company had changed so drastically since it was granted its franchise that there would be no alternative but to terminate its contract. Fortunately everyone was neatly lifted off the hook by the sudden availability of John Freeman, who had just given up his job as British Ambassador in Washington. Since he had been in the original prospectus as one of the company's main executives, his acceptance of the Chairmanship theoretically saved the situation, since the spirit of the original application, at least in terms of manpower, could be said to have been preserved.[30] Although a year after Freeman's appointment London Weekend had not produced anything more than routine programming, it had at least not accelerated its downhill process. That, at least, was something.

Life also became much easier for Brian Young and the commercial companies when the Government announced a cut of £10,000,000 in the advertising levy. Coupled with an increase in rentals, it still left them with another £6,500,000 of additional profit. Added to the cut in the levy of the year before, the companies were now set once more on the handsome profit trail. A lift in the economy and the growing use of colour in advertising brought sunshine to every company's financial statements. In 1971 television shares became one of the bright features of the stock market.

Indeed, so nicely placed had the companies become that they instigated a campaign to be given the fourth available channel. Running a smooth propaganda machine, Brian Young put up a plan which envisaged ITV-2 as a sort of watered-down version of BBC-2. There were promises of six hours of documentaries and features, two and a half hours of music and talk shows, three and a half hours of news. But the public was now immune to the rosy promises of aspiring television companies. And even the menu, although slightly more adventurous than the usual ITV diet, would hardly win any marks for novel or courageous thinking about the role of the medium.

Behind the companies' request, however, was clearly a move to forestall in the fourth channel the creation in 1976 of a rival commercial set-up. But scepticism about the companies' motives and future plans had set in hard amongst those interested in television. The view was that the companies might be on their best behaviour with this new channel until 1976, but once they had it firmly in their control, they would pump out the same sort of stuff that had diminished the over-all standard of British television since the commercial boys came on the scene.

An astonishingly virulent and aggressive swell of opposition to the proposals swamped the Minister for Posts and Telecommunications, Mr Chataway, and the Government. Almost unanimously, the press attacked the idea. So did academics and teachers. So did the trade unions. So did the Labour Party. In a debate on the proposal not a single MP on either side of the House thought that ITV should be given this vital national asset before an inquiry into the future of British television had been held. Even the advertisers and advertising agencies were opposed to it because they recognized that a strengthening of the companies' commercial monopoly position would enable them to demand greater advertising charges. It could be said that except for the executives of the television companies and a few civil servants, there was no one in the country who thought that the ITV could be trusted with a second channel at this particular stage.

Mr Chataway, who had seemed disposed to giving the companies their request at one stage, had to bow to this vociferous opposition. He rejected the companies' proposals, but to ease the ITV's discomfiture he announced an ending to the restrictions on broadcasting hours. With the opportunity to make profits with afternoon and early morning broadcasting, he had provided some salve with which the companies could heal their wounds. It was a humiliating defeat for Mr Young, and it revealed what suspicion and resentment ITV's past record had sown in the minds of nearly everyone concerned with the medium. If by 1976 the commercial companies had not demonstrated some greater awareness of the public interest than they had in the past, such opposition to any proposed extension of power would probably prevent them from getting another channel. And few people would shed any tears about such an eventuality.

CHAPTER IV

THE GREENE REGIME

He who prides himself on giving what he thinks the people want is often creating a fictitious demand for lower standards which he will then satisfy.— Lord Reith

In many ways the BBC of the late 1960s bore not the remotest resemblance to Reith's concept of broadcasting. The tone was different for a start. The note of lofty earnestness, sure of the cultural and spiritual benefits it was dispensing from an Olympian station in the sky, had given way to the chummy, raucous, rib-nudging, wheedling blandishments of the jester, the commentator, and the huckster. The dominant middle-class Oxbridge voice, with its overtones of assured superiority, had lost its grip on British television—though it still hung on in BBC radio—and had been replaced by a variety of regional, classless accents. The attitude of awed respect for the pronouncements of political leaders and Establishment figures had given way, in current affairs and some comedy programmes, to a sceptical and irreverent insistence on the right to submit such views to hard questioning and cynical mockery. The detachment from political and social controversy had been replaced by a belief in television as the right forum for them. The role of the high-minded teacher dedicated to guiding the nation towards loftier and worthier goals had been kicked aside for the part of a holiday-camp entertainer, enthusiastically whipping up the country into just another chorus, please, of *Knees Up, Mother Brown*. They were determined to prove that, when it came to show-biz entertainment—laughs, thrills, and spills—Auntie BBC was the sharpest impressario in the land.

'Auntie, as we all know, has taken to drink,' wrote Malcolm Muggeridge in the *New Statesman*, 'never goes to divine worship any more, gives noisy parties for disreputable friends and hangers-on, endlessly uses four-letter words, and to show how with-it she is, puts Jesus Christ on the cover of her Radio Times along with Che Guevara, Tariq Ali, Coco the Clown and other worthies.'[1]

Searching for the reasons for this drastic shift from the Reithian view of broadcasting, one can detect three significant influences. In the first place, post-war Britain, deprived of its Empire and baffled about its new world role, was out of sympathy with the omniscient voices emanating from Broad-casting House. These class-conscious accents and opinions struck a false note of complacency in a country increasingly uncertain of itself. When British attitudes and morals were being subjected to the pressures of change and doubt, it was incongruous of the BBC to go on behaving as if nothing had changed at all. Since the country itself was unsure of where it was going, it was impossible for the BBC to continue to act as if it knew the way.

The second important factor that forced the BBC to veer from its high-minded Reithian path was the advent of commercial television. Once the Corporation was forced to compete for viewers its freedom to impose tastes and values, rather than follow them, was seriously curtailed. If it did not compete vigorously for large audiences most of the time, the BBC was bound to dwindle into an elitist, minority service. If its audiences were to shrink too significantly then the question of its right to the entire revenue from television licenses—which had to be paid by everyone who possessed a set—would be questioned. Politicians would be bound to query the justice of demanding from all viewers the money to finance programmes few of them saw or wanted. In order to sustain its position as the major broadcasting organization in the country, and to justify the revenue that sustained it, the BBC had to ditch Reithianism as an impracticable and anachronistic luxury.

The third major influence in diverting the BBC from its inspiration and donnish posture was the appointment of Sir Hugh Greene as its Director General in 1960. Unlike his two post-war predecessors, the erudite newspaper executive and editor Sir William Haley, who ruled from 1944 to 1952, and the professional soldier Sir Ian Jacob, who held the job from 1952 to 1960, Hugh Greene was a professional broadcaster.

Born in 1910, Hugh Greene was the youngest of three brothers of remarkable talent and achievement. His eldest brother, Raymond, was one of the world's leading authorities on endocrinology, and his second brother, Graham, was the famous writer. Educated at Oxford, he became a foreign correspondent for the *Daily Telegraph* and reported the rise of Hitler in Ger-many until he was expelled in 1939. It is his boast that he was probably the first journalist in Warsaw to know the Second World War had begun: it was he who informed an incredulous Polish Government that the Germans were bombing Katowice.

He joined the BBC as Head of its German Service in 1940 and in the immediate post-war years was responsible for the broadcasting and dissemination of information to such places as the British Zone of Germany, Eastern Europe and Malaya. For two years before he became Director General he was Director of the BBC's News and Current Affairs. He was, therefore, when he took up the post, not only a pragmatic, hard-headed newsman and an expert on propaganda, but a veteran of twenty years of BBC affairs. No Director General before him —with the possible exception of Reith—had had such an intimate and intensive knowledge of the administrative by-ways and corporate philosophy of the world's largest broadcasting organization.

A large, tall man, Greene was like a benevolent lighthouse, beaming amiable chit-chat to anyone within range. But his courtly, almost diffident, manner camouflaged the existence of a tough thinker and a shrewd manipulator. As its Director General, Greene knew exactly what he wanted for the BBC.

'I wanted to open the windows and dissipate the ivory tower stuffiness which still clung to some parts of the BBC,' he has written. 'I wanted to encourage enterprise and the taking of risks. I wanted to make the BBC a place where talent of all sorts, however unconventional, was recognised and nurtured. . . .'[2]

When Greene took over as Director General, the BBC was already competing with commercial television for viewers. The real threat of this rivalry and its possible effects on the Corporation dawned only slowly on the BBC hierarchy. The early financial problems of the commercial companies may have engendered in the BBC a false sense of security about its television audience. Its monopoly on radio had left it singularly ill-equipped for a rough fight for popularity against a rival television organization. It had neither the personnel nor the inclination for such an unseemly brawl. By 1957, however, two years after ITV had come on the air, the BBC was truly worried.

According to Kenneth Adam, who subsequently became BBC's Director of Television for seven years, this concern was voiced by Gerald Beadle, Director of Television in 1957, when Adam joined the Corporation.

BBC television, Beadle warned me, was in a poor state. Wherever ITV had been established, notably in the London area, it was sweeping all before it. The whole future of public service broadcasting based on license revenue was likely to be called into question if the audiences continued to desert. . . .

BBC television seemed when I got there to be divided between those who were scared stiff of ITV and those who were intolerably complacent about it. . . . It took two years to pull BBC television into shape, and by then we were boldly putting out more serious programmes at the height of the evening than ever before, and three times as many as the competitor.[3]

Greene was by no means daunted by the prospect of competing for more viewers. He undertook the task with almost pugnacious relish. Unlike his predecessors who had thought of television as merely an extension of radio broadcasting, Greene recognized that the main battle for ascendancy in the media would be fought on the television front. If BBC television were to dwindle into an electronic whisper speaking only to the Happy Few, then the Corporation's influence on the affairs of the nation would become peripheral and academic.

The core of his problem was how to win popularity without risking the BBC's soul; how to provide entertainment without undermining the BBC's purpose; how to be a showman without sacrificing the moral, educational, and inspirational responsibilities of the medium.

His first task, however, was to prove to the Government and the country that the BBC's approach to broadcasting was the right one. The opportunity for presenting that case to a knowledgeable, objective tribunal came with the setting up of the Pilkington Committee on Broadcasting in the very year that Greene took over as Director General. Once such a Governmental body had given the Corporation its seal of approval, Greene could reasonably assume that his freedom of action would be secure for a number of years.

I approached this event, [wrote Greene] as a problem in psychological warfare: define one's objectives, rally one's friends, rattle one's enemies, state one's case with the utmost conviction, persuasiveness and clarity. . . . The ITV, led by the old victors of the campaign for commercial television in the early 1950s, made the usual mistake of thinking that they were fighting the same war over again and were bound to win. They were lazy in the public presentation of their case and fatally casual, even, I believe, contemptuous, in the preparation of their evidence, written and oral, for the Pilkington Committee. They got what was coming to them.[4]

In a speech given in 1963, Greene confessed that the enquiry had been an ordeal.

For two years or more it took up most of the time of many of us in the BBC. We had to marshal our evidence and our arguments. We had to think about ourselves and the justi- fication for our existence. . . . To have come through with success releases new energies—energies backed by all the thinking we have been forced to do about our responsibilities and our place in national life. So it was no coincidence that *That Was The Week That Was* came into existence at this particular moment and no coincidence that our programmes generally, from one angle or another, are trying to take a harder, franker look at *This Island Now*, trying to illuminate our national and international problems and our place in the world at this revolutionary time.[5]

How did the BBC 'justify its existence' to the Pilkington Committee? If the Pilkington Committee was right in com- mending the BBC for its philosophy of broadcasting—and no one condemned their findings on this issue—was the Corpora- tion justified in diverging from that philosophy to the extent that so many of its critics now claim it has? Indeed, has it diverged at all? Many of its executives and supporters indig- nantly deny that anything fundamental has changed in the BBC's broadcasting role over the past few years. Others have detected a lowering of standards, a decided shift towards 'giving the public what it wants,' an obsession with mass popularity inconsistent with its important public-service function, a readiness to convert television—and especially BBC-1—into a primarily entertainment channel not particularly distinguish- able in tone or content from its commercial rival. What, indeed, has happened to the BBC after Pilkington?

In its evidence to the Pilkington Committee the BBC sub- mitted no less than fifty separate papers totalling well over 150,000 words. They ranged across a wide field of technical, administrative, financial, and constitutional subjects. The hard core of its position on the past and future television policy of the Corporation was contained in five of these papers or memor- anda.*

Under Sir Hugh Greene's guidance, the BBC's aim was to show (a) that the Corporation had a fundamentally different

* They are contained in Volume 1, Appendix E of *The Report of the Com- mittee of Broadcasting*, 1960 (H.M.S.O., 1962). They are *Financing the BBC* (Paper 23), *Television: Serious Programmes in Peak Hours* (Paper 27), *Television Programme Policy in the Next Ten Years* (Paper 29), *Consequences of Competition in Television* (Paper 31), and *The ITA's Proposals for the Future of Television* (Paper 43).

programme philosophy from that of commercial television, (b) that the evidence of this difference was contained in the number of demanding or serious programmes transmitted at peak times, (c) that the quality, range, and quantity of these serious, demanding, and minority programmes, transmitted at peak times, proved its recognition of the responsibilities of public-service broadcasting, (d) that in order for it to cover an even wider range of serious, cultural, and informational programmes it should be given the right to run any new third television channel that the Government might authorize.

The object of these submissions was not merely to justify the BBC's programme policy but to belittle and condemn the programme policy of the ITA and the commercial companies. Nor did they mince words. The Corporation's attack on its rival's schedules and programmes is consistently aggressive, even contemptuous. Time and time again it dismisses with scorn any suggestion that the BBC and ITV were beginning to move in much the same direction—towards a greater emphasis on entertainment and popularity—and the accusation that there was now little difference between them.

The BBC cannot accept the claims that have been put forward in the past year or so to the effect that there is now a 'homogeneity' between the BBC and commercial television and that they are in large part 'assimilated.' On the contrary, there is in fact a marked difference between the character of the BBC's service and that of its competitors.[6]

And in a philosophical outburst, reminiscent of Reith in his more thunderous moments, it justifies its right to a second channel over the claims of commercial television, with these words:

All this is not to deny the energy, inventiveness, and determination sometimes displayed by some of the commercial companies. But the by-products of such enterprises are not often noticed at the time. No one intended that as a result of the industrial revolution in this country, which was a product of energy, inventiveness, and determination, and upon which our national prosperity depends, there should be created the industrial slums which are acutely embarrassing to the nation a hundred years later. Further opportunities handed to commercial television, especially if combined with a denial of such opportunities to public-service television, could create mental and spiritual poverty, which would be even harder to eradicate.[7]

To justify its firm assertion that there was a 'marked difference' between the Corporation and the commercial companies, the BBC relied mainly on the statistics showing that it consistently transmitted more serious and demanding programmes at peak-time viewing hours than its rival. But it recognized the problems of defining too dogmatically the categories of 'light' and 'serious' programmes.

What might generally be regarded as 'light,' e.g. 'swing' or the T.T. races, may be taken with the utmost seriousness by some people [it said]. Similarly, a Mozart opera, the purest form of relaxation to some people, may be regarded as all too serious by others. A serious message is often effectively conveyed by a playwright or by a variety artiste, for example, in a light or frivolous guise. . . . In measuring the balance between 'light' and 'serious,' it is unwise to be too categorical. . . . There is nevertheless a broad and useful theoretical distinction to be drawn between programmes that are in their nature and intention undemanding and those which inherently and purposely make a demand upon the intelligence and understanding of the viewer. In the latter category it is permissible perhaps to place such material as news and current affairs programmes, talks and discussions, documentary programmes, outside broadcasts of national importance, and other major events of a non-sporting character, music (other than 'light music'), opera, and ballet. Some plays undoubtedly fall into this category, though not perhaps all: it seems fruitless to attempt to divide all plays into one or other of two categories 'serious' and 'light.'[8]

As we shall see later on in this chapter, this relatively detailed account of what the Corporation meant when it referred to 'serious' programmes underwent certain modifications in the minds of television executives trying to justify the BBC's programme philosophy in the late 1960s. But it is the willingness to transmit a wide range of programmes that might generally be classified as non-light entertainment and non-sport that is the basis of the BBC's claim to greater responsibility than the ITV. And in their submission to Pilkington, they took that position one stage further. Such non-light entertainment and non-sports programmes had to be shown not in the very early evening and late night hours, but in the hours between 7 and 10.30 pm when the largest potential audiences were available to watch them.

It is the *core* [my italics] of the BBC's programme policy [says this memorandum] that its more important serious programmes should for the most part be offered when the largest audiences are available. . . . In the early years of competition, the commercial companies secured the larger share of the audience among viewers who could receive both channels, and they continue to do so. In the BBC's opinion, this result has been achieved by the programme companies by a process of concentrating on the less demanding types of entertainment during the main viewing hours.[9]

What sort of statistical balance, then, should be maintained during the peak hours for the BBC to fulfil its public-service responsibility? A survey covering the years 1958 to 1960 inclusive showed that of programmes transmitted between 7 and 10.30 pm, an average of 33 % (excluding drama) 'set out to appeal to the viewer's intelligence and make some demands on it.' By comparison, serious programmes made an average of only 11 % of what the commercial channel had shown during these same hours over the same period. For all hours, including its off-peak hours, the commercial network had transmitted about 17 % serious programming.

The Pilkington Committee in its final report had no reservations at all about which television service was behaving most responsibly and which balance they thought proper for the medium.

'We are left with no doubt that the BBC's concept of balance and quality is sound—both in the range and treatment of subject matter and in timing,' it said, firmly putting the imprimatur of official approval on the BBC's case. 'We are satisfied that within the limits of a single programme, the service in practice matches the stated concept of balance, and that, in a medium which has much to learn, the quality of their productions, though it can often be better, is generally good.'

The Committee's only reservation about the Corporation's evidence was a certain scepticism about its ability to resist the downward pressures of competition. Although the BBC had denied that competitive television had caused it to reduce—especially in peak viewing hours—the amount of more demanding programmes, the Committee was not so sure. 'We consider,' it wrote, 'that the pressure of competition has sometimes caused the Corporation, consciously or unconsciously, to depart in practice from its own ideal of public service broadcasting.'[10]

The Committee's findings on the record of the ITA were scathing. They flatly rejected the Authority's philosophy that television was merely a mirror of society, that it could not seriously shape or influence the values and attitudes of society, that life in the future would be much the same—with or without television. They denounced the commercial channel's concept of balance, which they said did 'not satisfy the varied and many-sided tastes and interests of the public.' They even criticized—unkindest cut of all—commercial television's light entertainment, which they said lacked quality. And they were of no two minds about ITV's responsibility for the widespread belief that television was trivial.

'The disquiet about and dissatisfaction with television are, in our view, justly attributed very largely to the service of independent television,' read its stern summing up of the commercial channel's performance. 'This is so despite the popularity of the service, and the well-known fact that many of its programmes command the largest audiences. . . . We conclude that the service of independent television does not successfully realise the purposes of broadcasting as defined in the Television Act.'[11]

The BBC, and particularly Sir Hugh Greene, reacted with understandable satisfaction to this vindication of their policies. 'The BBC emerged from the enquiry more successfully than we had imagined in our wildest dreams,' said Greene. 'Everything was there that we had hoped for, or very nearly everything. It was an exciting moment. Perhaps when one looks back one is tempted to think that we did almost too well. But one does not fight a campaign to achieve a partial victory.'[12]

To demonstrate its approval of the BBC's record, Pilkington recommended that the Corporation should be given as soon as possible a second television channel. Its disapproval of the ITV was voiced in its recommendation that it should not receive an additional television channel so long as it was constituted and organized as it was. It suggested a change in the structure of commercial television, whereby the ITA would receive all the avertising revenue and would be responsible for the general planning of the schedules. The companies would merely produce programmes to sell to the ITA and would have no direct access to money from advertising.

In effect this would have converted commercial television into another centrally controlled body like the BBC, differing only in its method of finance. Naturally this was totally unacceptable to the Conservative Government within whose ranks were many fierce supporters of ITV. Because the recommendations were stated in such general terms, and the actual details of how the ITA would function under this new constitution were not spelt out in any precise way, they were easily ridiculed and demolished both in the press and in the Commons.

In addition to the impracticability of the Committee's plans for a new type of commercial television, the harshness of its criticisms of the commercial channel produced an angry backlash. A typical reaction was that of the Tory Postmaster General, Reginald Bevins, who was at the time engaged in trying to introduce a levy on the scandalous profits being amassed by the companies. Even though he knew something had to be done about commercial television—particularly with regard to its financial structure—he thought the Pilkington Committee had gone much too far.

> I myself felt at the time that the Pilkington Report was unbalanced in its strictures upon commercial television and had given far too much weight to the views of the 'do-gooders' whose opinions, rather than the opinions of the public, seemed to have dominated the minds of the Pilkington Committee. I also believed that the acceptance of Pilkington would have destroyed commercial television. I did not want that for I happen to believe in competition. . . .'[13]

It might be noted that in deciding not to alter the structure of commercial television the Government did not pay much attention to the Pilkington Committee's suggestions about the quality of television and what it might be doing to society. Since the Committee had provided *no* concrete evidence that television's influence was anything more than ephemeral, politicians would be reasonably unperturbed by any suggestions that serious changes were necessary.

The BBC, however, was faced with the exciting challenge of setting up a second television channel of its own. In April 1964 BBC-2 made its debut. Because it was transmitted on a UHF Band and a 625-line standard, whereas the two older channels were still transmitted on a VHF Band and 405 lines, it meant that anyone wanting to see the new channel had to purchase a new television set. Under such circumstances, it was clear that BBC-2 was going to take some time before it ever became a serious competitor for audiences with BBC-1 and ITV.

The new channel made its first mistake by too rigidly determining to be different. Each night of the week was to be devoted to separate types of viewing. Tuesday would be educational, Wednesday would be a night of repeats of the best shows from BBC-1, Thursday would be specialist and minority orientated. Mondays and the week-ends would have most of the light entertainment and drama shows, but Sundays would be suitably serious. This plan, however, was soon abandoned.

'I thought that the idea of special programmes for different days of the week was a good one,' Sir Hugh Greene told me a few months after these changes were made. 'Wrongly, I now realize. It clearly wasn't. But people ought to put up with a certain amount of experiment. I think the demand for instant success is unreasonable.'[14]

Nevertheless the public could not be blamed for the expectations roused by the Corporation's publicity machine. The press reacted favourably at the time, and the highbrow label which was inevitably hung round the neck of the new channel has never been eradicated. Although its schedule began to take on a more orthodox shape, with programmes planned as alternative viewing to what was being transmitted on BBC-1—so that a serious programme on BBC-1 was balanced by a light one on BBC-2 and vice versa—the BBC's hierarchy never allowed the young channel to blossom out on its own, or to achieve a ratio of serious to non-serious programmes similar to that of BBC-1.

BBC-2's reputation as a repository of more demanding and more minority programmes than the senior channel has always been zealously maintained. As BBC-1 became more and more involved in a tussle for ratings with the commercial channel, the existence of BBC-2 as the conscience of the Corporation became vitally important to those justifying BBC-1's preoccupation with popularity. To anyone who complained that BBC-1 was becoming on many evenings indistinguishable from ITV, the glowing worthiness of BBC-2 could be adduced to prove that the Corporation had not lost its public-service soul.

Freed from the conventional limitations imposed on programmes made with one eye on the ratings, BBC-2 in its first five years under Michael Peacock and his successor, David Attenborough, produced some of the best television ever made in Great Britain. There was the twenty-six-part series, each episode an hour long—culled from a treasure of Allied and German film archives—showing the causes, the progress, and the end of the 1914–18 war. Called simply *The Great War*, it recorded this momentous conflict with a degree of historical objectivity, visual excellence, and sense of drama hitherto unknown in the medium. As an epic documentary, *The Great War* had done something never before achieved by either the cinema or television.

The adaptation of John Galsworthy's Forsyte novels into a twenty-six-part, hourly serial called *The Forsyte Saga* resulted in one of the most successful series ever transmitted on British television. Every week, millions of viewers shared the genteel tribulations of this upper-middle-class family. Produced for BBC-2, and proving an even greater success when transmitted on BBC-1, the young channel demonstrated by this series what a treasure trove of programme material existed in the popular English novels of the past. Another considerable achievement in television terms, which would probably have never been attempted by either BBC-1 or the commercial network, was *Civilization*, a thirteen-part, hour-long series in which the art historian Sir Kenneth Clark gave his interpretation of man's cultural progress as he saw it reflected in the masterpieces of sculpture, painting, and architecture.

In the field of humour, too, BBC-2 came up with some fresh notions. The series *Not Only . . . But Also* with Peter Cook and Dudley Moore brought a fresh brand of intelligent whimsey to the small screen, and in *Q.5* and *The World of Beachcomber*, Spike Milligan provided illustrations of the more delectable brands of British anarchic and nonsense humour.

Determined also to live up to its pledge to satisfy the needs of large minorities, BBC-2 introduced regular programmes like *Wheel Base, Horizon, Music International*, and the *Money Programme* which catered specifically for the tastes of those interested in motor cars, science, music, and money. One of its very few crusading programmes—BBC-2 output has been surprisingly free of political commitment and controversy—has been *Man Alive*, which at first veered too obviously towards sensationalism in its treatment of social deviants such as homosexuals and child murderers, but which in its later years settled down to a conscientious examination of a large number of pressing social issues. Another novel idea, which one would never have seen on the senior channels, was *Europa*, in which Derek Hart regularly surveyed with a knowledgeable and sardonic eye selections from European current affairs and documentary programmes.

Yet in spite of providing some of the most popular programmes that have ever come out of the BBC—*Forsyte Saga, Not Only . . . But Also*, and in the early 1970s, *The Six Wives of Henry VIII*—BBC-2 has never succeeded in living down its highbrow image. By the end of 1970 over three-quarters of the population pos-

sessed sets capable of receiving BBC-2. It had a potential viewing audience of 25,000,000 people. Yet its programmes rarely
managed to attract even 5 % of the total viewers, and its ratings
were so disappointing that seven years after it went on the air
the Corporation would still not issue any statistics on the size of
its audience.

The reason for this failure of the second BBC channel to pick
up a large following was that it could never match the consistent
record of BBC-1 and ITV in producing light entertainment or
sports programmes. The television viewer is notoriously resistent
to change and generally loathe to exercise any choice about
what he is going to watch.

As one will see later on, it is useful for BBC-1's competitive
position *vis-à-vis* ITV that BBC-2 continues to remain a
cultural ghetto. By relegating some of its public service responsibilities to the junior channel, BBC-1 can indulge in the
ratings game with more freedom and, hand on heart, can claim
its total television output is more serious than ever before.

The creation of BBC-2 was not, however, the Corporation's
only reward for winning the Pilkington Committee halo of good
conduct. Even more important was the freedom of action which
such a verdict assured. Sir Hugh Greene interpreted Pilkington's blessings as a green light for the plans he had always had
for making the BBC a harder, franker, fresher, more sceptical
reflection of the nation's activities.

Some of these changes had been introduced before Pilkington
and Greene's appointment as Director General. The nightly
programme *Tonight*, produced by a pugnacious young Welshman, Donald Baverstock, was a vivacious television magazine
that bubbled with passion and humour. It exposed scandals,
commented on the news, raised controversial issues, mocked
authority. In the late 1950s it was already a sign of the things to
come. Its zest and irreverence was a decided contrast to the
converted, static, and dogged radio shows—*The Brains Trust,
Asian Club, Twenty Questions, At Home*—which made up so much
of the BBC's television schedule. Without the acclaim won by
Tonight, the more controversial satire shows could never have
been conceived. And the young team of producers that made
Tonight possible—Baverstock, Alasdair Milne, Ned Sherrin,
Anthony Jay—were to be responsible for the programmes that
shocked the nation a few years later.

'He caused the BBC, by precept and example, to forget the
thirties, with their severe paternalism,' was how the BBC's
Director of Television, Kenneth Adam, summed up Sir Hugh's

influence in the early 1960s, 'the forties with their narrowed objectives and restricted activities, and the fifties, with their ex-regular officers in charge, their squabbles between radio and television, and their apprehension of the competitor. He rallied the top team, after purging it, and drove a faintly incredulous but increasingly enthusiastic staff into a brave acceptance of the sixties. "It is not the BBC that has changed but Britain," he said, but he was wrong. With him in command Auntie BBC changed its sex, and for the first time in its life was young.'[15]

It is easy to exaggerate the revolution that took place under Hugh Greene's stewardship. Trying to provide 6,500 hours of television every year, it was inevitable that most of those hours would be filled by programmes that were second-rate and predictable. Genius is no more common in television circles than any other walk of life. For most viewers the liberating influence of Hugh Greene meant little. They watched the BBC for *Grandstand*, *The Black and White Minstrel Show*, *Top of the Pops*, *Come Dancing*, *The Billy Cotton Band Show*, *Dr Finlay's Casebook*, *Perry Mason*, *Dr Who*, *Dick van Dyke*, *Rolf Harris*, *Val Doonican*, and they were contented enough.

This kind of undemanding entertainment—genial, relaxing, familiar—made up the bulk of BBC programmes during the nine years of Greene's regime. It did so before he arrived and does so now. The programmes that are identified with the Greene era, which aroused so much controversy and gave the BBC an entirely fresh image, are relatively few in number. They are to be found in the field of current affairs, where programmes like *Panorama* and *Gallery* took on a sharper, more abrasive tone in their scrutiny of the political scene; in the late-night satire shows like *That Was The Week That Was*, *Not So Much A Programme More A Way of Life*, and *BBC 3*; in the *Wednesday Plays* like 'Cathy Come Home' and 'Up the Junction'; in the strikingly original comedy series *Steptoe and Son* and *Till Death Us Do Part*.

There can be no doubt that the so-called satire shows shattered once and for all the assumption that the BBC could be counted upon to support all the traditional, assured, Christian, middle-class, Establishment values of the Corporation's past. According to Kenneth Adam, the notion of satire on television was conceived by himself and Hugh Greene and was enthusiastically taken up by the brilliant and ruthless young men who had learnt their trade on the topical television magazine programme, *Tonight*—Donald Baverstock, Ned Sherrin, and Alasdair Milne. 'Our idea of political satire was based on our varying experience—in Berlin in [Greene's] case, and in London in mine—of the thirties,' wrote Adam. 'Their idea was sharper, more cruel and compassionate, bang up to date.'[16]

Nothing like *That Was The Week That Was*, transmitted late on Saturday nights, had ever been seen on British television before or, for that matter, on television anywhere else in the world. Making its bow towards the end of 1962 and aimed at a sort of topical revue of the week in skits and songs, its audacity and effrontery sent part of the nation into hysterical giggles, while another part of the nation was sent reeling for its smelling salts.

Not only was nothing sacred to *TW3* but the taboos of decades were suddenly and unceremoniously booted into oblivion. Millions stayed up late on Saturdays to watch with astonished glee the unprecedented spectacle of living politicians being mercilessly abused, religion being ridiculed, authority being derided, and sexual aberrations being openly exploited for laughs. There was a Consumers Guide to Religion in which Christianity was treated as so much soap powder. There was a *This Is Your Life* of the Home Secretary, Henry Brooke, which described him as 'the most hated man in Britain' and ended with the line 'If you're Home Secretary—you can get away with murder.'

There were skits about dirty films and fly-buttons and illegitimate children and Labour Party advertising. ('I cannot tell new Instant Wilson from old pipe-smoking Attlee. P.S. I can't tell new Instant Wilson from old stab-in-the-back Wilson.') Some of it was scintillating; much of it was jejune and amateurish. '*TW3* was a breakthrough into bad taste which was a constructive criticism of the ghastly good taste that preceded it' was how that perceptive critic T. C. Worsley described the programme's particular quality.[17] About 4,000,000 viewers began watching it. After eight months something like 12,000,000 viewers—an unheard-of audience for a show that went out close to midnight—were expectantly tuning in for their weekly electronic shock.

Protests about the show flooded the BBC. After a particularly vicious attack on Sir Alec Douglas-Home, who had succeeded Harold Macmillan as Prime Minister, it appeared the programme could not possibly survive. With a General Election looming in 1964 it was clear that politicians—particularly the Tory Government—could not be expected to tolerate this sort of abuse much longer. Inevitably *TW3*'s run was terminated at the end of 1963 instead of continuing on into the spring as had been originally intended. But the Director General, Hugh Greene, was at pains to point out that this decision did not mean he had lost confidence in the *TW3* team. It was purely the imminence of the election that had brought about the curtailment of the show's run.

Once the election was over—and Labour back in power with a tiny over-all majority of five seats—Sir Hugh Greene, true to his word, brought satire back to the BBC. This time there was much more of it. On Friday, 13 November 1964—just a month after election day—a monstrously-sized programme, lasting for 45-minutes on three consecutive nights, sprawled across the weekend like a voluptuous, winking madame. Called *Not So Much a Programme More a Way of Life*, its aim was a combined chat show and revue which would cast an oblique and irreverent eye on the events of the week.

The attempt to mix conversation and comic skits, to blend serious comment with flippant clowning irritated more viewers than it delighted. With David Frost presiding over incongruous collections of guest speakers—professors shared the discussions with politicians and comedians—the level of talk tended to sink to a facetious common denominator. Commentators were selected because they were slick rather than wise, glib rather than articulate, indifferent rather than impartial. Inevitably some of the sketches and chat went too far in either content or language. Considering the fact that the shows were live and the temptation to make outrageous remarks to score a point or get a laugh was so great, it is surprising how few serious mistakes of judgment were made in this unwieldy show.

A skit about a Liverpool priest urging a working-class woman to have more children made a first-class row. The use of the word 'cretin' by Bernard Levin to describe Sir Alec Douglas-Home almost swamped the BBC's switchboard with complaints. An operatic version of the events leading to the Abdication of Edward VIII was transmitted at a moment when the Duke of Windsor was ill and the Princess Royal had just died; in the event this rather affectionate piece was villified as another example of the show's horrific bad taste.

In spite of the increasing volume and intensity of criticism against the BBC for allowing these satire shows to go on, Sir Hugh Greene staunchly continued to defend them. To him, they represented conclusive proof that the Corporation was decisively not the orthodox voice of the Establishment.

I think these programmes have been an enormously

healthy development in the BBC [he told me in an interview late in 1964]. I cannot understand people who write about *TW3* and *Not So Much* as if they were some sort of excrescence of the BBC's that we are merely tolerating.

Of course, if we didn't have programmes like *Panorama*, *Tonight*, and *Gallery*, we would be unjustified in putting on *Not So Much*. But it is a supplement to these other features and looks at current affairs through fresh and sceptical eyes. *TW3* and *Not So Much* were nurtured and encouraged at the highest levels in the BBC.

I think enormous prestige has been accumulated by the BBC throughout the world because of *TW3*. It was seen everywhere as an example of the independence of the BBC from Government control. This reputation for freedom and our national ability to take criticism does the BBC good and the country good.[18]

But soon after that bold affirmation of support, Sir Hugh was issuing an official apology because of the affront caused by the birth control sketch. In March 1965 *Not So Much*'s run was prematurely terminated. Few mourned its passing. The programme's indiscretions had provoked anxiety among the BBC Governors and certain important executives.

Even the excesses of *Not So Much* did not, however, completely kill off satire on the BBC. In descending order of wit, competence, and point there were programmes like *BBC3* in 1966, *The Late Show* in 1967, and *The Eleventh Hour* in 1968. They still made derisory jokes about politicians ('Speculation is rife that Harold Wilson is suffering from strange instability. He likes to hear himself described as Her Majesty the Queen.') They still had their scandals. On *BBC3*, Kenneth Tynan's use of the word 'fuck' in a discussion of censorship gave the nation a mild fit of apoplexy. They still could be vicious and cruel as *The Late Show* in its clumsy attacks on Anthony Eden and Somerset Maugham.

But though there were still some very clever and witty talents inspiring these shows—John Bird, Eleanor Bron, John Fortune, John Wells—their attacks seemed arbitrary and erratic. The early satire shows, tearing away at long-established taboos and hallowed shibboleths, seemed to many to be the needed expression of the destructive, cynical force that followed the thirteen years of Conservative rule, the Profumo scandal, and the aftermath of Suez. But those people were less keen on seeing that same cynicism at work on the Labour leaders and the so-called new Britain that had presumably come into being in the middle sixties. The climate of tolerance was fast passing and the satire boys soon felt the chill wind of tighter control and official supervision. Under such conditions, it was natural that their spontaneity and assurance should be weakened. Before the 1960s were out, satire programmes had vanished from the BBC schedules.

Along with satire, as evidence that the BBC under Sir Hugh Greene was determined to shock and disturb viewers into a recognition of the changes that were taking place in Britain, was a series of regular 75-minute plays called the *Wednesday Play*. Edited by James MacTaggart, these plays were rarely comfortable, easy, or conventional. Not only did they tackle themes such as abortion, bad housing, political corruption, schizophrenia, but they dared to shoot them in an experimental fashion that was confusing to viewers familiar with the cosy, straightforward techniques of conventional television directors. In plays like 'Cathy, Come Home,' 'Up the Junction,' 'In Two Minds,' produced by Tony Garnett and directed by Kenneth Loach, the blend of videotape and film, the use of documentary techniques, and the speed and verve of the editing created a TV drama that could rouse millions to a recognition of such social scandals as the treatment of the homeless, back-street abortions, and callous mental hospitals. The assault on pre-conceived notions of what television plays should be about, the involvement with sordid and complicated issues, the readiness to distort the truth for a passionate dramatic effect, all provoked vociferous resentment in those who saw the BBC as a rampaging Goliath, ready to trample upon all the cherished attitudes of the past.

'The BBC faced its biggest public censure yesterday after Wednesday's television play *Up The Junction*' ran a news story in the *Daily Mail* on 5 November 1965. 'It received a record number of protest calls from viewers. The first of hundreds came three minutes after the play started. The protests continued coming in throughout the night and all yesterday.'

It was not only BBC satire and the *Wednesday Play* that upset traditional viewers. Two comedy shows, *Steptoe and Son* and *Till Death Us Do Part*, succeeded in the double feat of rousing passionate opposition and becoming the two most popular shows transmitted by the Corporation. *Steptoe and Son* was resented by many because its central characters were dug out of the lowest and sleaziest strata of British life. Although classic comedy has constantly used the humblest characters to comment on the ludicrous nature of the human condition (Shakespeare's clowns, the good soldier Schweik, Charlie Chaplin, Beckett's Estragon, all have this function) television comedy series have almost always dealt with mild, amiable, and middle-class figures.

Steptoe and Son was, on the contrary, set in an unashamedly ugly milieu. Its heroes were a wheedling, cunning, sneering old man and his assertive, day-dreaming, bachelor son who made their living by collecting scrap. Their experiences with lavatories, sex, politics, money, were recounted with relish, gusto, and uninhibited language. Beneath the obvious vulgarity was a disturbing look at the hypocrisy of family relations and a telling comment about the claustrophobic and destructive nature of contemporary life. The expletives, the sexual innuendoes, the squalor shocked many viewers into indignant protests. But their anxiety was not taken very seriously by the Corporation. In 1965 *Steptoe and Son* attracted 8,000,000 viewers weekly, getting higher ratings than *Coronation Street*—the most popular series in British television history—which opposed it on the commercial channel.

The complaints about *Steptoe and Son* were but a placid ripple compared to the storm of protest roused by Johnny Speight's Alf Garnett, the monstrous hero of *Till Death Us Do Part*. Like some boil on the back of the neck that one cannot resist stroking, this working-class social aberration demanded the nation's attention. In 1966 and 1967 some eighteen million viewers—half of Britain's adult population—watched him in a weekly series that wallowed in the hates and fears and prejudices most of us have tucked away in some genteel niche in our psyche. Not only did the squalor of the setting match that of *Steptoe and Son*—an East End slum house with an outside toilet —but the scruffy Alf Garnett, tieless, baggy-trousered, moustache dripping with beer foam, yelling expletives and obscenities, magnified in a hilarious but disturbing way all that was narrow, intolerant, vicious, and crude in the English character.

Alf's views on coons, kikes, and wogs, expressed in just those words; his reflections on the Labour Party; his suspicion of anything new like transplant operations; his ignorant superstitions; his insensitivity to beauty; his blatant hypocrisy, were all the more pointed and relevant because they could be seen and heard most days in most pubs, factories, and boardrooms in Britiain. Alf's defence of Christianity and his loyalty to the Queen were expressed in such blunt, stupid, and vulgar arguments that Christians and monarchists were quick to repudiate any suggestion that someone so crass and so vulgar could possibly be on their side. Indeed, there were loudly-voiced suspicions that Alf Garnett had been invented by the BBC to undermine and belittle just those right-wing, loyalist, and religious values he was professing to admire. It should be said in the BBC's defence that *Till Death Us Do Part* was not a one-sided affair. To balance Alf Garnett's ignorant prejudices were the views of his son-in-law, a left-wing, lazy lout whose arguments on behalf of the workers and intellectuals were just as cliché-ridden and crude as those of the monstrous Alf. To justify its view that the complaints about Alf Garnett represented the opinions of only a tiny minority of viewers, the BBC could point to the fact that *Till Death Us Do Part*, being seen by half the adult population, was the highest rated show in the country and the most popular comedy programme ever transmitted by the Corporation.

While the satire shows, the *Wednesday Play*, and the comedies were being hailed or denounced as evidence of a markedly different direction being taken by the BBC, they never amounted to more than a miniscule proportion of the Corporation's total television output. Out of the total 6,500 hours being broadcast each year, these controversial programmes probably made up not more than 2 % of the television schedule. It is important to recognize when considering what changes were actually taking place in BBC programming that the vast bulk of shows— sport, education, variety, old films, American series, comedy— were untouched by this fresh trend. Except for the two comedy shows and a few programmes of *That Was The Week That Was*, the broadcasts that were being debated so hotly by protagonists and opponents of the BBC's policy were never seen by the bulk of BBC viewers. Over 75 % of the potential audience went to bed before most of the satire shows were on the air and an even greater number would never knowingly have switched on to the *Wednesday Play*.

The argument, therefore, that raged in the middle 1960s about what the BBC was up to was carried on by articulate minorities, all claiming the support of the nation. Taking an almost impish pleasure in suddenly finding itself accused of being a disruptive irritant rather than a soothing balm in British society, the Corporation summarized in its annual handbook of 1966 some of the criticisms and praise that had been heaped upon it during the year in what it called 'the lively debate about the BBC.'

A chapter headed 'The BBC: Focus of Controversy' quoted

Ian James of the *Catholic Herald*, and indirectly myself, as two voices for the defence.

While I regret and deplore the BBC's occasional lapses I also thank God for its courage. If the BBC was to play it safe, to confine itself only to cosy, uncontroversial pap like *Coronation Street*, *The Black and White Minstrels*, and quiz shows it might have a peaceful time from the watchdogs, but it would be impossibly dull and unstimulating broadcasting. And it would also be failing in its duty to cater to all sections of the public. . . . I share the view of that distinguished television critic Mr Milton Shulman that 'it is a positive duty for the BBC to put on programmes that occasionally shock, disturb, and anger.'

A leader in *The Guardian*, quoted in the *BBC Handbook*, took much the same line.

It is true that the BBC genuinely outrages a minority of viewers because it presents what they do not want to see or hear, or would prefer not to know about, in a deliberately disturbing way. More exactly, the dramatists, the journalists, the theologians of the current decade have deliberately questioned the complacency around which so much of our cosiness has been built. Worse, some of them have laughed at it, and the BBC, a founder-member of the Establishment, has connived at mocking the Establishment.

Few would deny that this is the authentic spirit of the time. What, then, is the BBC to do about it? To blur over the sharp edges of our social discontents, of our religious questionings, of our frustrations in human relationships? That, in effect, is what the Clean-Up TV campaign is asking, and that is what the Director General refuses to do.[19]

The spearhead of the attack on the BBC was, however, organized by a self-appointed vigilante body called, at first, the Clean-Up Television Campaign and which was later converted into the more authoritative-sounding National Viewers' and Listeners' Association. It owed its birth to the alarm of two Birmingham housewives, Mrs Mary Whitehouse and Mrs Norah Buckland, at what they felt certain programmes were doing to young people. Mrs Whitehouse and Mrs Buckland drew up a manifesto which they hoped would be signed by about 4,000 people and which they would send to the Corporation.

The manifesto asserted that its supporters believed in a

Christian way of life and deplored present day attempts to belittle and destroy it. 'In particular we object to the propaganda of disbelief, doubt and dirt that the BBC projects into millions of homes through the television screen,' it read. 'Crime, violence, illegitimacy and venereal disease are steadily increasing, yet the BBC employs people whose ideas and advice pander to the lowest in human nature and accompany this with a stream of suggestive and erotic plays which present promiscuity, infidelity and drinking as normal and inevitable.' It finally called for a radical change of policy and for programmes which would 'encourage and sustain faith in God and bring Him back to the heart of our family and national life.'[20]

When this petition was presented to Parliament in June 1965, it had 365,355 signatures. They had been accumulated through the efforts of Mrs Whitehouse and her supporters, and included the names of MPs, a number of Chief Constables and senior Churchmen. The BBC, with a propaganda expert like Sir Hugh Greene at its head, was not likely to remain passive very long under this rain of abuse. The Corporation quickly mounted counter-offensive tactics of its own. In order to prove that Mrs Whitehouse's women only represented a fraction of female public opinion, they took their case to the representatives of large national women's organizations. Mr Kenneth Adam, the BBC's Director of Television, wrote a letter to the *Church of England Newspaper* on 7 August 1964.

'You may be interested to know that delegates from 15 official and national women's organizations, representing more than ten million women, recently attended a conference arranged by Miss Doreen Stephens and myself,' said Mr Adam. 'What they had to say about BBC television was very different from what we hear from Mrs Whitehouse.'

Thus after seven years as Director General, Sir Hugh Greene could feel that he had helped push the BBC right into the centre of the swirling forces that were changing life in Britain. And that, by its interest, the BBC was not merely reflecting and recording these changes but was helping to agitate them as well. His views of what the BBC was doing at this time are contained in a lecture he gave at Birmingham University in October 1968, in which he attempted to sum up what had taken place at the BBC during his years as Director General.

I think the BBC's output during those years (ITV, with its safe formulas, played a much smaller part in this) has brought out into the open one of the great cleavages in our society. It is of course a cleavage which has always existed: Cavalier versus Roundhead, Sir Toby Belch versus Malvolio, or however you may like to put it. But in these years was added to the split between those who looked back to a largely imaginary golden age, to the imperial glories of Victorian England and hated the present, and those who accepted the present and found it in many ways more attractive than the past. It was not a split between old and young or between Left and Right or between those who favoured delicacy and those who favoured candour. It was something much more complicated than that, and if one could stand back for a bit as the brickbats flew it provided a fascinating glimpse of the national mood. It also provided at times a rather distressing insight into the degree of sickness and insanity in our society.'[21]

There were, however, inexorable forces closing in on Greene which were determined to subdue this questioning, provocative spirit of the BBC and also to cut down the individual power of the Director General. At the beginning of 1967, although pursued and harrassed by politicians and pressure groups, the BBC reached the apex of this controversial phase in its history. In its current affairs programme, it defiantly resisted all the direct and indirect pressures being brought against it by the Labour Government. In the field of satire, although quality had deteriorated and brilliance was at a premium, there was still the *Late Show* mocking aspects of religion and authority. In drama, the *Wednesday Play* was still frankly and imaginatively dealing with social problems involving sex, poverty, lunacy. In the light entertainment field, the ignorant, foul-mouthed, intolerant Alf Garnett of *Till Death Us Do Part* was delighting half the nation.

When Greene gave up his job as Director General two years later, in March 1969, the determination of the BBC to include programmes that provoked and shocked was much less in evidence. A creeping conformity, a growing reluctance to cause trouble, a greater emphasis on light entertainment and sport on BBC-1, were signs that the foundations of the Greene regime were being gnawed away by orthodox wood-worm even before he was gone. The process accelerated with almost indecent speed once he had vacated his office and left the destinies of the BBC to Chairman Lord Hill, and the succeeding Director General, Charles Curran.

Although the concept of public service and the support of minority interests were firmly imbedded in Sir Hugh Greene's broadcasting philosophy, he was always keenly conscious of the BBC's competitive position and its need to justify its existence by acquiring a large proportion of the viewing audience. He felt that if, without lowering standards, the BBC could win 45% of the national audience against the ITV's 55% that would be a respectable achievement.

Policies must of necessity be interpreted by individuals. The balancing act between public service and popularity was primarily performed at the BBC by the head of BBC-1. The importance he gave to competition, the twist he gave to the schedules, the emphasis he placed upon the entertainment side of television played a major part in setting the tone and spirit of the BBC's television service.

Although quite different personalities, the three heads of BBC-1 during the 1960s—Donald Baverstock, Michael Peacock, and Paul Fox—shared a desire for competitive success against their commercial rival. They also had in common the fact that they were schooled in the news and current affairs departments of the Corporation, and were all relatively young—under forty—when they took over their jobs. In the curious hierarchical ladder of BBC administration, the heads of both television channels were several rungs below the Managing Director of Television, and the Director of Programmes, Television. But it was the heads of BBC-1 and BBC-2 who were closest to the actual creative roots of the television operation.

The first head of BBC-1 under the fresh administration set-up that came into being with the formation of BBC-2 was a stocky, garrulous, argumentative Welshman called Donald Baverstock. Ideas bubbled out of him with volcanic intensity. He talked at a staggering clip—metaphors, historical allusions, and anecdotes tumbling out with breathless irrelevance. 'He would take forty minutes,' said a colleague, 'to explain the need for silence.'

He was the first to know that out of every ten ideas he threw up, nine were impossible. But he expected them to be argued about and analysed, at least as a basis of discussion. He took some understanding, and in the BBC he infuriated some and inspired many.

It was Baverstock's push and drive and journalistic flair that made *Tonight* and *That Was The Week That Was* two of the great production landmarks of the BBC. He was, also, very conscious of the ratings struggle with commercial television, and was exceedingly impatient with those who felt that the Corporation should be above such mundane considerations.

Donald Baverstock, who resigned after an administrative row, was succeeded by the 38-year-old Michael Peacock, head of the still evolving BBC-2 channel. His sudden promotion to chief of the largest programme producer in the world left him almost breathless. 'I'm the most surprised man in the world to be in this office,' he told me in an interview at the time. 'Donald's pictures are still on the wall and that's his diary on the desk.'[22]

Using phrases like 'the need to be conscious of broadcasting and not narrowcasting,' Peacock, too, was keenly aware of the new competitive imperative that had gripped the Corporation with the arrival of commercial television. Putting the squeeze on ITV by scheduling light entertainment against any serious programmes transmitted by the commercial companies was in his view a justifiable tactic for gaining more viewers. And he could see that the existence of BBC-2 as a receptacle for most minority programmes made it easier for him to use that tactic.

One of Peacock's main contributions to the BBC's competitive posture was a greater reliance upon old feature films. Until 1959 British television had been unable to buy films that had been shown in the cinemas. The British film industry, terrified of the growing popularity of the small screen and worried by declining audiences, had taken the Canute-like stand of buying up all available feature films simply so that the BBC and the ITV could not transmit them. However, this ludicrous attempt to stop the inevitable was undermined when the BBC brought off a secret deal to purchase one hundred films from RKO. The one feature film a week which had been shown in the early 1960s tripled during the Peacock regime.

By agreement, no film could be shown earlier than five years from the end of its round on the British cinema circuits. Because so much more money and technical skill had gone into the making of these films, they possessed production values that few television programmes could match. Their popularity, however, proved stultifying to the creative and artistic development of television. Since these films had usually recouped their costs in cinema distribution, they were relatively cheap. They could be repeated with each showing, thereby becoming progressively less expensive. Films could be bought that cost as little as a fifth or even a tenth of what it would cost to mount an original play or an episode of a television series. The schedules filled by old films meant that much less opportunity for fresh ideas and thinking in the medium. It encouraged laziness and complacency on the part of television executives who could always fill an empty spot with the repeat—even a second and third repeat—of a popular film like *Room At The Top* or a John Wayne western.

The increasing use of old films, which in Peacock's era rose from one to three a week—and later under his successor, Paul Fox, increased to seven and eight a week on both BBC channels—may have provided economic relief to the BBC's ever chronic finances but it certainly played a major part in preventing television's expansion as a different and more imaginative medium than the cinema. In most Western countries television has become largely a midget-sized distributor of old films. The BBC might have resisted this trend. But economics and the desire for popularity encouraged it to rely upon the film industry as a cheap, predictable, and safe source for electronic fodder.

After only two years as chief of BBC-1, Peacock resigned to join London Weekend as its Managing Director. Into his shoes in June 1967 stepped Paul Fox, whose career in the BBC had included six years as editor of *Sportsview*—the Corporation's main sports programme—and a number of years as editor of *Panorama* and as head of the BBC's Current Affairs Department. A burly, shrewd man with neither the panache of Baverstock nor the articulate reasoning power of Peacock, Paul Fox's record as an inspirer of programme ideas or as an innovator of fresh approaches to the medium has hardly been noteworthy. Except in the field of sport, which he has encouraged to a preposterous degree, Paul Fox's major achievements lie in his ability to manipulate a schedule and to capture audiences by picking the weak points—i.e. the non-light entertainment programmes—in the commercial channel's output and opposing them with more popular offerings. His approach to his task seems to be that of a master chess player. He has been given certain pieces—*Panorama*, a weekly documentary, a play, sport, variety, serials—and he deploys them in a way most likely to win the ratings game. Explaining his job in an interview, Mr Fox said:

> There are two or three big sessions in a year known as the Offers Meetings when Head of Output Groups and Output Departments will come and offer X, Y and Z in particular fields. They will know in advance how many productions I can take, how many plays I can take, how many documentaries I can take, how many comedies I can take. It's up to them to get on with it. They're powerful people, that's their job. We discuss the question of money and lengths and facilities and so on, but the content of what goes into the

Wednesday Play, what goes into the *Tuesday Documentary* is up to those chaps who are running the Departments. I would not dream of interfering with them.[23]

In other words, it was the mix that was Fox's main concern, and, of course, it is the mix that ultimately determines the tone, spirit, and purpose of a broadcasting service. The BBC's concept of the mix and its distribution throughout the schedule was the primary issue by which the BBC convinced the Pilkington Committee of its superiority to commercial television and of its primary role as provider of public service broadcasting.

Obviously the personality of the Controller of BBC-1 could also affect the quality of those individual programmes about which he was particularly interested. Just as Baverstock's presence and involvement helped shape the nature of the satire shows so, no doubt, did Peacock's expertise influence current affairs programmes and Fox's background impress itself upon the quality of the sports coverage. No head of a BBC department, conscious of the interest of his immediate superior in his field, would be very happy in his job if he was not sensitively aware of the taste and attitudes of men like Baverstock, Peacock, or Fox. It was, therefore, not altogether surprising that under Paul Fox the BBC went sports mad.

CHAPTER V

ANYONE FOR TENNIS? HORSE-RACING? FOOTBALL? CRICKET? ATHLETICS? SHOW JUMPING? BOXING? GOLF? WRESTLING? ETC.?

If the French noblesse had been capable of playing cricket with their peasants, their chateaux would never have been burnt.—G. M. Trevelyan in *English Social History.*

The numbers both of hard core gamblers and compulsive gamblers had at least doubled in the past ten years. And the average age has lowered in that time.— The Rev. Gordon E. Moody, Secretary of the Churches' Council on Gambling, 1972.

She was a hunched, tiny, working-class woman in her late sixties. Every day you could find her in the same London betting shop putting a few pennies on the horses. One day she turned up dressed in black.

'What's happened?' one of the shop's regulars, a taxi-driver, asked her. 'Why the black?'

'Oh, I'm burying my husband this afternoon,' she said. 'But I've just got to have a bet first.'

This true anecdote epitomizes the English passion for sports and gambling. The sports mania and gambling fever that characterizes so much of contemporary British life has a long and honoured history. The diversity of sports and the manner in which all classes participated in them has been described by the historian G. M. Trevelyan. Back in the seventeenth century, for example, while the gentry enjoyed their hawking, deer and fox hunting, netting of birds, the common folk, too, were enthusiastic followers of many games.

'Other popular sports were wrestling, with different rules and traditions in different parts of the country; various rough kinds of football and "hurling," often amounting to a good-natured free-fight between the whole male population of two villages,' writes Trevelyan. 'Single-stick, boxing and sword-fighting, bull and bear baiting, were watched with delight by a race that had not yet learnt to dislike the sight of pain inflicted. Indeed, the lesser sporting events of hanging and whipping were spectacles much relished. But cockfighting was the most popular sport of all, on which all classes staked their money even more than upon horse-racing.'[1]

Foreigners have continued through the ages to be baffled and bewildered by the Englishman's earnest and passionate involvement in sports. Pierre Daninos, the French author, lightheartedly recounts how in the 1950s on a visit to London he saw a newspaper headline reading 'ENGLAND'S DESPERATE POSITION.' Since M. Daninos was very worried about the international situation at the time, these words naturally alarmed him. He was relieved, however, to learn that the 'desperate position' of the nation was due to her having lost by 6–3 a football match to Hungary for the first time in ninety years. Even in such adverse conditions, the newspaper had not lost all hope in the country's future. According to M. Daninos, a sub-head read 'In spite of 6–3 be proud of old England.'[2]

With sport imbedded so firmly in the national psyche, it is inevitable that television should devote a great deal of time to it. But the recent history of British television, particularly the BBC, indicates that the broadcasting authorities have not been so much catering to a need as exploiting it. Because sport fits so easily into an entertainment-oriented use of the medium— it is for the most part an undemanding activity easily comprehended by large groups of viewers—it is a natural complement to variety, quiz games, domestic comedies, action-adventure series, and old films, as a means of filling schedules dedicated to frivolity and amusement. Since sport is the leisure activity about which most people in Britain care most intensely, it is relatively easy to whip up passionate minorities—sometimes very large minorities—for almost any game. Television has managed over the years to create substantial followings for such relatively minor sports as show jumping, ice skating, all-in wrestling, boxing, golf, athletics, swimming, motor-cycle racing, rugby. It has made football a national religion. It has turned cricketers and tennis players into stars rivalling in popularity the best-known figures of stage and screen. In short, it has changed sport for vast numbers of viewers from a leisure activity to an obsession. Once a fringe aspect of Britain's social life, sport now makes very significant demands on the people's time, concern, emotions, and financial resources.

This raising of sport to the level of a top national priority has been achieved by television devoting thousands upon thousands of hours—a large percentage of them at peak time—to various types of games. Under the guidance and inspiration of Paul Fox, a former TV sports editor who became BBC-1's Controller of Programmes in 1967, the incursion of sports into the BBC's schedules—and by electronic osmosis, into the life of the nation—has reached unprecedented proportions.

From the Corporation's standpoint there are obvious advantages in relying upon sport to fill up a substantial segment of its schedule. It is relatively easy to organize. It is less expensive generally than mounting such alternative peak-time programmes as a play or a variety show. It is something that the BBC has done much better than its commercial rival and it therefore clings tenaciously to its lead in this field. Attempts by the commercial channel to arrange some agreement for sharing or alternating between channels the transmission of national sporting events, so that unnecessary duplication would be avoided, have been firmly resisted by the BBC. 'Alternation is exclusion' is the doctrine adopted by the BBC to justify its dubious judgment that the public interest would best be served by having both channels televising the Cup Final, Wimbledon, or the Boat Race. Who else but *Pravda* and *Izvestia* plan their coverage together, said Paul Fox, invoking a thoroughly irrelevant comparison to vindicate the BBC's right to transmit as much sport as it liked whenever it liked.

The event that changed the BBC's reasonable approach to sport to an obsession with it was undoubtedly the series of World Cup football games in July and August 1966. In a planning decision unique in the history of television, the Corporation turned over an entire three weeks of most of its peak-time schedule to football. Its justification for the swamping of the box with a single sport was the argument that the World Cup finals were taking place in England for the first time in forty years. I called it at the time an 'arrogant and indefensible decision,' and said that this 'wanton disregard of audience preferences would be very costly to the BBC in the long run.' I could not have been proved more hopelessly wrong.

By an incredible twist of luck, England won the World Cup in 1966. As they progressed from quarter-finals to semi-finals to finals, viewing figures zoomed until it seemed that the entire nation was transfixed by the spectacle and the hope that England would be once more acclaimed as the land of the best footballers in the world.

Having established its ability to do what the commercial channel could not do—acquire massive ratings through sport—the BBC pressed home its competitive advantage in this field and devoted more and more of its available hours to games of every description. In 1968 it was the Olympics in Mexico that received similar saturation coverage. From October 12 to 27, the Corporation transmitted over two hundred hours of live and recorded programmes about the games. Split between BBC-1 and BBC-2, this represented an average of almost *fourteen hours a day of athletics*! On BBC-1 you could see the Olympic games in programmes at 7 am, 12.30 pm, 5 pm, 6.20 pm, and 9.55 pm.

One might have thought that such a concentration on the Olympics would have induced the planners to give a little less time to other sports so that some other aspects of British life might receive a reasonable representation on the small screen. Not at all. In 1968 the BBC proudly announced they would be televising the Winter Olympics at Grenoble; the Test Matches between Australia and England; Wimbledon Tennis; the Open Golf Championship; the Amateur Boxing Championships; Motor racing; international athletics; The National Swimming Championships; women's hockey; Rugby Union games; swimming between Britain and Canada; the Royal International Horse Show; the Horse of the Year Show.

These programmes were in addition to the BBC's regular weekly sports programmes—*Grandstand*, *Sportsview*, and *Match of the Day*—and such national events as the Derby, the Boat Race, the Grand National, and the Football Association Cup Final. This bonanza of sports coverage totalled over a thousand hours of muscular display in a single year—over one-fifth of BBC-1's total output.

When the World Cup finals came round again in 1970 the BBC naturally assumed it was its public duty to whip up the nation into a frenzy about its football team in Mexico. This time, however, the event coincided with Britain's General Election. There was not the slightest indication that anyone in the BBC hierarchy thought it might be in the national interest to concentrate the electorate's mind during these few weeks on the political issues facing them, rather than on the winning or losing of a football title. There was no move to curtail the extensive plans for blanket domination of the screen by soccer. In the first week of the campaign, the BBC transmitted four times as many hours of World Cup as it did of news and information about the General Election. In the week of the election itself—both Sundays inclusive—BBC-1 provided no fewer than thirty-one hours of football. The commercial channel produced nineteen hours of the same thing. Most of that time England wasn't even in the competition since they had been beaten by West Germany a week before. 'A national disaster' was how a BBC commentator described this defeat.

It is interesting to compare British coverage of the World Cup with that of West Germany who actually reached the finals. Although there was no General Election on in West Germany, that country did not feel that its football feats needed more than a total of sixteen hours TV coverage on its two channels. Britain, on the other hand, devoted fifty hours to an event in which it was no longer participating and at a time when one might have thought responsible TV would wish to interest the country in its impending political future.

'On the morning after England's defeat in the World Cup,' I wrote in the *Evening Standard* on 8 July 1970, 'I heard for the first time in pubs, shops and garages people actually talking about the cost of living, trade union reform and the relative merits of the main parties.

'For the first two weeks of the election campaign a large slice of the electorate was living in a fantasy world in which the winning of the World Cup was far, far more important than entry into the Common Market, the balance of payments, lower taxes, the future of trade unions and comprehensive schools, the choice of the rulers of their country. . . . For a sports-mad nation of which it was once said that the millenium would have to be postponed if it interfered with Henley, the hysteria and preoccupation with football at a moment of vital national decision was something truly remarkable and humiliating.'

Amid all the explanations of why Labour lost the 1970 General Election against all the predictions of pundits and polls, there is a growing consensus view that Harold Wilson's attempt to run a no-issue campaign was a major tactical blunder. His faith in a 'trust-me-I'm-your-leader' approach to the electorate might have worked if the voters could have been diverted from thinking too much about the election. Whether the dates of the World Cup had anything to do with Wilson's timing of the election has never been established. But coinci-dence or not, the take-over of the small screen by football during the vital weeks of the campaign fitted in neatly with the Labour leader's strategy to underplay the issues and rely upon the image of the miracle man who had broken the balance-of-payments problem and who would enable Labour to coast to victory.

Unfortunately for Wilson, the public was only ready to be

mesmerized by soccer so long as England was winning. But the cold douche of defeat four days before polling day suddenly turned many people away from the euphoric notion that any country must be in a healthy and sound state if it could turn out the best football team in the world.

'The defeat in the World Cup was the jar—the first terrible breach of the myth on which we were floating,' said ex-Labour Minister, Richard Crossman, in a radio discussion diagnosing Labour's defeat. This view of a nation sleep-walking its way through a moment of important decision-making was expressed by a number of foreign observers reporting on the election. Although it is impossible to prove, I suspect that if England had still been in with a winning chance on 18 June 1970, Labour would have been returned to power.

The power of television to affect an election through its sports coverage is something that is not likely to happen very often—if ever again. But what this speculation is meant to demonstrate is the ability of the small screen to inculcate false values and unreal expectations through the enshrinement of sport as a way of life.

Nothing better illustrates television's capacity for arbitrarily creating a whole set of fresh enthusiasms and hero figures to be admired and emulated by the public than the BBC's treatment of show jumping. In most other countries, the training of horses to jump over a variety of obstacles has a minuscule following of people with enough money and time to become proficient in this very expensive, exclusive game.

It would be safe to estimate that in France, Ireland, Russia, and Italy—to name only the countries that competed in 1971 in the European Horse Trial Championships, won by Princess Anne—99.99% of the people could not name a single prominent figure in their show-jumping worlds.

But thanks to the BBC's relentless covering of these events, riders like Harvey Smith, David Broome, Marion Coakes and horses like Stroller and Manhattan have almost as many devoted followers as the biggest names in football and cricket. And when a Royal princess achieved prominence in a sport which the BBC had lifted from obscurity to national significance, the Corporation could barely restrain its genteel hysteria. Said the sports writer J. L. Manning of the *Evening Standard*, describing the television account of Princess Anne's triumph in the European Championships, 'Dorian Williams on BBC made us feel the poor girl was not so much about to become the Royal Family's first European champion as enter Westminster

Abbey. He had the organ playing and the massed choirs singing.'

There is, of course, an inevitable tendency for televised sports to be puffed up and enthused over by commentators because the very act of televising such an event involves the transmitting organization in its success. Unlike sports writers who can report to their readers that a game was boring, dire, or below standard, the television commentator tends to hail the most mediocre achievements as classical feats of perspiration. If the games are too bad, they are blandly explained away with discreet excuses and polite understatements. This is probably natural because, acting as an electronic impressario for such an event, the BBC or ITV must feel bound to justify its choice to the viewers. In other words, the very act of transmitting an event, having enthusiastically publicized it, inhibits the transmitting organization from objectively assessing its true merits. If they confess it was a dull and disastrous game, they are confessing that they have been offering the public dull and disastrous TV entertainment.

Because there is this commitment to a game's entertainment value, it becomes difficult for commentators to utter many words of deprecation or disapproval about an athletic occasion. Not only does this unalloyed enthusiasm distort the event, it devalues true achievement by assuring sports enthusiasts that the third-rate is something to be admired and applauded.

This capacity to be awesomely adulatory about the prowess of sportsmen often reaches absurd heights of chauvinism whenever British players are in competition with foreigners. Support or admiration for one's national or regional team gives a competitive edge and zest to life which can be both stimulating and enjoyable. But when patriotic zeal so blinkers criticism as to blur the public's assessment of real athletic merit, false values replace genuine ones. Sports commentators in press or broadcasting are notoriously unrestrained in their language, but those in television are unmatched in their ability to interpret a sixteenth place in the downhill slalom or an early elimination in an Olympic trial as a national achievement. If, as it is argued, this approach merely typifies the traditional English philosophy that it is the game that matters more than the winning of it, then it is hypocritical of these same commentators to react to a British victory as proof of national superiority.

There was a time when BBC TV programmes lifted into prominence such a variety of diverse figures as the archaeologist

Sir Mortimer Wheeler, the painter Sir Gerald Kelly, the philosopher Professor Joad. By showing them displaying their skills and erudition in discussions or enlightened quiz games— often at peak times—they cultivated, particularly amongst the young, a curiosity and interest in their professions. But since BBC-1 went pop there has been little time or place in the Corporation's prime-time schedules for programmes that encourage the public to admire personalities of solid, academic, or creative achievement. Instead, this important channel concentrates something like 20% of its time on building up amongst the young an enthusiasm for kicking balls, developing muscles, riding horses. Only a fraction of that time is concerned with developing minds, stimulating discussion, encouraging questions about moral and social values. By its indiscriminate and undue emphasis on sport, the BBC presents an unbalanced picture of life in Britain. If, as a consequence, many young people get their social priorities wrong, can we not detect a probable TV factor in that process?

Of course, if British television is deemed to be primarily an entertainment medium, sport may be said to be preferable to silly quiz games, banal chat shows, repetitive domestic comedies, violence-saturated series and old films. To counterbalance its inculcation of false values, it can be argued that sport stimulates commitment to a communal activity, inspires a concept of loyalty, encourages respect for physical prowess, cultivates a desire for good health, channels and drains off aggressive and violent instincts. For all these reasons, sport, of course, should always be given a substantial proportion of available television time. But it should not be given so much attention that it encourages an unhealthy preoccupation with it and diminishes awareness of the other activities life has to offer. As I have stressed repeatedly in this book, it is all a question of the mix. The Corporation in the late 1960s and early 1970s has, in my opinion, got the mix seriously wrong.

But if it is impossible to quantify in any meaningful way the harm or benefit a society derives from an intense involvement with sport—and television is responsible for much of this involvement—there is one area of sporting activity influenced by television which definitely leads to undesirable consequences for a large number of people. That area is gambling. Although the English will bet on anything—General Elections, beauty contests, flies climbing up a wall—it is horse racing that stimulates the greatest gambling fever. In 1970 ten times more money was bet on horses than on football pools or bingo. The question any reasonable society ought to be asking itself is whether gambling on the scale now seen in Britain is something that can be viewed with equanimity or something that ought to be discouraged.

As a moral issue, British Governments have decided since 1960 that gambling could never be curtailed or stamped out by legislation. In that year the Betting and Gaming Act was passed, setting out rules to regulate rather than to prohibit it. By this piece of legislation the Government conceded that the social consequences of gambling were not deleterious enough to continue any attempts to prevent it. The Act brought in its train hundreds of gambling clubs, thousands of betting shops, tens of thousands of jackpot machines. So acceptable had gambling become by 1968 that the Government thought it proper to encourage national savings by a monthly lottery in which the holders of Premium Bonds would be eligible for large prizes derived from the interest moneys that these savings would have accumulated at an annual rate of $4\frac{1}{2}\%$ tax free.

This opening of the flood gates to gambling not only took much more money out of the economy than had at first been calculated, but the infiltration of Mafia elements to get some share of these lucrative pickings and the subsequent rise in crime forced the Government to take steps to discourage this nasty trend. A process of severe taxation and strict licensing-controls reduced the number of gaming clubs in Britain from 1,056 in 1968 to only 123 in 1971. Attempts were also made to discourage gambling on horses by the introduction in 1966 of a $2\frac{1}{2}\%$ betting tax on turnover, raised to 6% on off-course betting in 1969. Although these taxes on every bet—only deducted by bookmakers on winning bets—made it virtually impossible for any consistent horse-gambler to make any long-term profit out of his gambling, the actual turn-over reported by bookmakers in 1970—no less than £1,172,852,000—was higher than in 1967 before these heavy taxes were introduced. In other words, taxation has proved singularly ineffective in dampening the nation's determination to bet on horses.

Now it might have been thought that two enterprises like the BBC and the ITA—deriving their authority and revenue from State monopolies—would have deemed it their responsibility to express the Government's concern about the increase in gambling. If they did not produce programmes aimed at discouraging gambling habits, it might reasonably have been assumed that any bodies professing to have the public interest at heart would not have produced programmes that positively encouraged them. But in their treatment of horse-racing that is precisely what the British television organizations have done. Indeed, they have competed with each other in devising schemes to get more and more people into the betting shops. Television has been the bookmaker's best friend.

If television were to confine its horse-racing coverage to the major races of the year and a straightforward report of a few races on Saturdays and holidays, its duty to racing-enthusiasts would be reasonably served. But British television goes far beyond such a restrained service to the betting industry. For events like the Derby and the Grand National the BBC organizes programmes stuffed with details about the horses, jockeys, and trainers which are guaranteed to whip up as much enthusiasm as possible for these annual gambling sprees. Knowing that nothing is going to stop the British having a flutter on these big races, the Corporation behaves as if it had a responsibility to satisfy the public's whim to lose money.

While one may view with a certain indulgence, television's build-up of enthusiasm for such big racing events as the Derby, the Grand National, the St Leger, the Guineas, it is quite another thing when its routine racing coverage is so extensive that it encourages a growing number of the population to indulge in gambling almost every day of their lives. Almost every Saturday one can view ten races on both major channels, and during the week there is likely to be one or two other race meetings transmitted on the box. Although it trails behind the BBC in most aspects of televised sport, when it comes to horse-racing commercial television is now forging ahead. Its ration of seven races on Saturdays beats the BBC's three, and its all-year coverage is greater in volume than that of the Corporation. On a national Bank Holiday like Whitsun, the British public can be stimulated into betting on no less than twenty-two races, thirteen on Saturday and nine on Monday.

Any bookmaker will tell you that the greatest boon to his business has been the televising of races. On days when racing can be seen on the small screen, there is a formidable leap in the volume of betting. This phenomenon of substantial increases in gambling associated with TV racing has also been seen in America.

As if that were not service enough to the bookmakers, both the major channels have been devising schemes to get more and more viewers hooked on betting. This obsession with the gaming aspects of horse-racing is a far cry from a decade ago when the BBC never provided any betting odds on the air. If you enter any betting shop in Britain you will see prominently displayed posters urging customers to try their luck at finding the ITV 7 or the BBC Triella. This type of bet is also recommended in the advertisements of all the major bookmakers.

And small wonder. These bets are the type of sucker bets most likely to turn bookmakers into millionaires. They are basically accumulator bets depending upon a sequence of winning horses to recover a profit. The commercial channel has been most irresponsible in the manner in which it has enticed viewers to gamble. It made a great play of its ITV 7 which demanded nothing more nor less than finding the winners of all seven races televised by ITV. As a practical achievement—finding seven winners in a row—it is far more difficult than winning the Jackpot which is a large reward for picking six winners in a row. If a professional tipster on a newspaper 'goes through the card'—which means recommending the winners of all six races at a meeting—it is usually front-page news. Yet the commercial channel urges its viewers to take on a bet which can be won only against impossible mathematical odds.

When they first introduced the bet, the commercial channel showed us rooms filled with gold bullion which would have been won had you succeeded with the previous week's ITV 7. Although such blatant incentives to losing money are less evident today, the encouragement of gambling goes on. After each race the accumulated winnings that might have been won are statistically recorded on the screen, and the commentators breathlessly inform us that there are still a few possible winners around after the first five or six races. These usually fail to get the lot. Indeed, with a rare display of guilt, some bookmakers have agreed to pay out some fraction of this impossible bet if four or five winners are found. It is, of course, in their interest to keep the public plugging away at this formidable goal. 'Last week you could have won £53,539 for 10 pence on the ITV 7,' read a bookmaker's advertisement. Notice the words 'could have won.' The perniciousness of this kind of betting incitement lies in the fact that there must be many weeks when not a single soul in the land has won the ITV 7. The entire amount wagered has gone into the bookmakers' tills without a penny being returned. This could not happen on the football pools where a substantial proportion of the total amount wagered is returned every week to the winners, nor in bingo where winners must always be found. Thus commercial television has lent itself to a device which not only stimulates betting fever but provides the smallest return of any gambling investment in the country.

Not to be outdone by their rival's success with the ITV 7, in 1971 the BBC introduced Triella. This is an accumulator bet which merely requires the finding of the first and second horses in all three races televised by the BBC on a Saturday afternoon. Again this is an awesome feat, unlikely to be accomplished by the most clairvoyant gamblers, and guaranteed to pour riches into the tills of bookmakers. At the Cheltenham meeting in March 1972 the BBC, with a straight face, reported that for a ten-penny wager the Triella had returned £225,024. They did not say that anybody had won it. If anyone had, we would surely have been told.

In the 1972 report of the Churches' Council on Gambling, *The Facts About The Money Factories*, The Rev. Gordon E. Moody had this to say about the TV bet, 'The broadcasts emphasise the betting, giving as much attention to bookmaking as to horse-racing. . . . Betting of this kind is generally the most profitable for bookmakers. The odds are so astronomical that the vast majority lose.'

Now one of the central moral and political dilemmas of a free society is how far the State should go in imposing restraints on an individual's freedom of choice. It is easy, for instance, to decide that heroin should be banned; it is less easy to decide that marijuana should be banned. In the interests of the welfare of the State (laws against murder, violence, theft) and even in the interests of the convenience of the State (parking regulations, limitations on road speed and drinking hours) a free society does not grant an individual total freedom.

When, however, the State discovers that some activity that has hitherto been unrestricted is causing serious suffering and heavy wastage of manpower and money, it usually takes steps to regulate that activity or discourage it. Although people are still free to smoke themselves to death, Governments in countries like Britain and America have not only engaged in expensive public-relations exercises to point out the hazards of smoking but have also introduced legislation insisting that health warnings be printed on every packet of cigarettes. Another regulation that has been considered necessary is the prohibition of all cigarette advertising on television. The fact that no such prohibition exists about newspaper advertising is a tacit recognition of the far greater influence that television has on people's habits than newspapers.

In a similar way it can be argued that, while it is not a

Government's responsibility to prevent people squandering a large share of their income backing horses, there might come a moment when betting had reached such proportions as to bring about costly and unhealthy repercussions on the body politic. According to some competent authorities, that point had been reached in 1971. While a Royal Commission on Betting, Lotteries and Gaming, surveying the British betting scene in the years 1949–51, concluded that there were no serious social consequences due to gambling at that time, the liberalization of the gaming laws had brought about a more disturbing situation twenty years later. The very fact that the Government had to introduce more restrictive gambling legislation in 1968, as well as impose heavy taxes on general betting, indicates that the social consequences of unfettered gambling were too serious to be allowed to continue.

The main arguments against the excessive amount of gambling in Britain in 1971 were that too much money was being spent on it, too much time was being wasted on it, and too many people were becoming compulsive gamblers. If we examine just one of these gambling consequences—its over-all cost—we can see why television ought to be actively engaged in discouraging rather than encouraging gambling mania. With over 14,500 betting shops and large telephone-account bookmakers like Ladbrokes, William Hill, and the Tote, employing almost 100,000 people, the total cost of financing this vast complex of gambling enterprises, together with the betting tax, cannot be far short of £300,000,000. All these facilities and taxes and bookmakers' profits can only be paid for in one way—by lost bets.

The Churches' Council on Gambling has estimated that there are about one million persistent gamblers in Britain. At a rough guess such gamblers must be losing sums ranging between £3 to £6 a week. If there are a million people—mostly workers—losing sums of this nature, ought a Government to be concerned? What is the impact of such regular losses on wage demands? Is this merely a minimal drain on the economy or a significant contribution to inflation?

'Gambling today is overgrown and overheated beyond genuine demand as a result of a decade of vigorous and widespread commercial exploitation,' wrote Mr Moody.[3] Since the incidence of betting increases substantially when races are televised, and since stunts like the ITV 7 and the BBC Triella have become part of the means by which the bookmakers attract fresh gamblers into their shops, there can be little doubt that the small screen has inadvertently been a tremendous help to those engaged in the 'vigorous commercial exploitation' of gambling.

Should anyone doubt the mesmeric power of television to raise the volume of betting, let me quote Mr Moody once again. 'One of the developments advocated to increase betting is a system of closed-circuit colour television provided from the course for betting offices. The Editor of *Sporting Life* thought the effects of this would be so dramatic (29 October 1970) that bookmakers would be willing to pay (though it seems highly improbable) the sum of £2,000 on average per betting office for such a service—a total of £28,000,000 a year.'[4] On a limited scale—and beamed into homes rather than betting shops—that is precisely the service that the BBC and the ITV are providing bookmakers, free of charge.

The question roused by the sports coverage on British television is not whether it should be shown in reasonable measure but whether too much sport, by monopolizing too much of a limited national communications asset, results in the presentation of an unbalanced view of British life. Surely it must be part of the function of those responsible for broadcasting to ensure that the television organizations do not behave like giant dope peddlers doing their best to fix the nation on some sort of powerful illusion about togetherness and happiness through sport.

In addition to encouraging the wasteful and dispiriting practice of gambling by its over-zealous transmissions of horse-racing, television, by stimulating the mania for sport can drive a nation like Britain more and more inward until its bogus achievements in games becomes an adequate substitute for more valuable endeavours. If England wins the World Cup what does it matter if it has lost its influence in the Middle East?

As a nation, there are plentiful signs that Britain is becoming more insular and petty in her approach to international affairs. Even if the country appears to be drifting to the bottom of the second-rate-power league, one gets the impression that few people will care if they are compensated on television by a victory over the Hungarians at ping-pong. And the youth of the land, through the box, are being led to believe that ten artists like Henry Moore do not equal one boxer like Henry Cooper or that a hundred scientists like Alexander Fleming are no equivalent for one footballer like George Best.

In a highly industrialized society like Britain where technological advances are going to make the satisfactory filling of leisure time an even more pressing problem, it is obvious that sport and games of all kinds should be taught and encouraged. And television is uniquely fitted for such a task. But an over-indulgence in sport, as this chapter has tried to show, can ultimately be more harmful than beneficial. It seems about time that the hierarchy at the BBC and the ITA began to relate the over-all output of sport to the national interest so that the people's natural appreciation of sport will not be distorted to an indiscriminate passion for petty heroes or lead to an unthinking acceptance of third-rate achievements.

CHAPTER VI

WHO CAN TELL THEM APART?

I don't know where television is heading but I do know that it seems on the whole rougher, cheaper, shoddier, dirtier, nastier and more vulgar than it need be, and than it used to be.—Maurice Wiggin in *The Sunday Times*, 26 September 1971, summing up his experience after twenty years as the paper's television critic.

It was the mix, the melange, the mosaic of the Corporation's output that was in Paul Fox's hands from June 1967 onwards, and in his hands it underwent some significant changes. Soon after he took over he indicated that he intended to give ITV a much tougher battle for viewers and that he was particularly keen on changing the 60 to 40 ratings lead that the commercial channel had on Sunday nights. A further edge to the ratings battle was provided by the fact that a new company, London Weekend, was to come into being in the autumn of 1968, and Fox was determined to clobber them as ruthlessly as possible in their earliest days. Since London Weekend was now run by Michael Peacock and a number of other former BBC executives, there obviously would be some special relish in showing them how effective old Auntie BBC could be in the popularity game if she really put her mind to it.

In less than a year Mr Fox had managed to make the BBC on weekends as much a receptacle for light entertainment shows and old films as ITV. The shift towards sport and non-serious programming was also evident during the weekdays.

It would be misleading to attribute too much of this shift of programme emphasis to Paul Fox's presence at the summit of BBC-1. A much more significant appointment also took place at the Corporation just a month after Fox's elevation. Harold Wilson's decision to make Lord Hill the BBC's Chairman was to have a far more important influence in halting and even reversing Sir Hugh Greene's effort to give the BBC a questing, probing, analytical role in the nation's affairs. As we have already seen, the Labour Prime Minister recognized in Lord Hill a fellow politician whose career at the Independent Television Authority had shown he could understand politicians' problems and would uphold a concept of balance which in essence meant neutralizing rather than increasing the impact of television. If in the process of making sure that the BBC made less trouble for politicians, Lord Hill also dampened down its new-found zest for querying social issues, ridiculing accepted shibboleths, satirizing venerable institutions and Establishment figures, broadening the area and language of TV debate, the new Chairman was not likely to find much opposition or resentment from politicians of any party.

Lord Hill, who took over as Chairman on 1 September 1967, soon made his presence felt. It was clear early on that he was going to be far more active in delving into the details of programmes than had other Chairman before him. Particularly if those details were in the delicate and controversial area of 'good taste.' According to Kenneth Adam, who was Director of BBC TV at the time, Lord Hill's first active intervention of this sort was prompted by a line in the song 'I Am A Walrus' from the Beatles film, *Magical Mystery Tour*. The offending line was 'Crab a locker, fishwife, pornographic priestess, boy, you been a naughty girl you let your knickers down.' Hill wanted the line to be eliminated or the programme cancelled altogether.

Sir Hugh Greene refused to do either. In view of what Greene and Adam had been supporting in the satire shows, this indication of their new Chairman's 'decency' threshold must have been a chilling portent of what was in store for the BBC. Lord Hill threatened to issue an 'instruction.' Sir Hugh held his ground. It was fairly firm ground since it was discovered that Radio One was already broadcasting the offending lyric twice a day. When the film was shown, not a single viewer claimed to have been offended by the song.

Other examples of the change of bureaucratic temperature at the BBC after Lord Hill's arrival were listed by Kenneth Adam in a series of articles in *The Sunday Times*. There was Hill's demand that the BBC apologize for the use of the phrase 'dirty Jewboy' in an episode of *Softly, Softly*. He wanted the apology to be broadcast in or before the news. Greene's deputy, Oliver Whitley, resisted this demand and the row was settled by a placatory statement when the next episode of the series was shown.

In Adam's view, the Governors, now including some new members, were becoming increasingly cautious and sensitive about the contents of programmes. 'Was there not too much girding at authority in current affairs programmes?' was the kind of question they began to ask. 'Did not certain plays give unnecessary offence?'[1]

On one occasion Adam, with three of his colleagues, was

called before the Governors to answer accusations that there had been an excessive portrayal of sex in one play and that there had been too many 'bloody's in a play by John Mortimer. In Adam's opinion it was not a satisfactory meeting. He was particularly disturbed by the Governor's concentration on the tiny percentage of plays that were superficially controversial and their refusal to balance these against the vast number of BBC plays which were classical, traditional, or replete with happy endings.

It was in this atmosphere of caution, second thoughts, anxiety about the BBC's radical and permissive image that the Board of Governors decided to set out its thoughts on BBC broadcasting policy. In Adam's opinion, this document would never have been written had both he and Sir Hugh Greene and a number of other senior members of the Corporation's Board of Management not been in New Zealand attending a Commonwealth Broadcasting Conference. The writing of this encyclical, originally designed as a guide to senior staff, revealed the tug-of-war for the soul of the Corporation that was going on between those who felt that the BBC's new freedom and morality had gone too far and those who felt that this fresh enquiring spirit was right. The document was circulated among governors and directors and re-worded to include as many as possible of the varying splinters of opinion in the higher echelons of the Corporation. 'What finally emerged was emasculated and philistine, but at least we had staved off disaster,' wrote Kenneth Adam.[2]

Issued in July 1968, and called *Broadcasting and the Public Mood*, this product of compromise had the tone of courageous caution, assertive neutrality, conservative liberalism, adventurous good taste that confirmed to many that under Lord Hill the BBC was certainly going to change. In the press the document received a generally chilly and sceptical reception.

A year after Lord Hill's arrival the BBC's programme output was certainly less disturbing to politicians, less irritating to the Establishment, less offensive to the clean-up groups. The satire shows were over and there was no suggestion that they were ever coming back. The last series, *The Eleventh Hour*, had had a short run early in 1968, but the sparkle, the fun, and the irreverence of its predecessors was missing. Was it, as some suggested, that the vein of inspiration had been exhausted or that a climate of reticence, caution, and disapproval at the top was creating an atmosphere inimicable to the production and writing of uninhibited satirical programmes? The current affairs programmes like *Panorama* and *24 Hours* had lost their bite and crusading zest and were less ready to subject public figures to hard questioning. The shocking and popular comedy series *Till Death Us Do Part* was off the air, and the plays were becoming more innocuous and conventional.

In an organization like the BBC no directives or memoranda are needed to bring about a change in direction, a deceleration of pace, a deviation in approach. Good executives are adept at seeing invisible writing on the wall, catching intangible straws in the wind, hearing inaudible sounds in the air. No threats, no orders, no commands are given, and yet miraculously the whole organization takes a detour and marches in step—with a few exceptions—towards a different goal. Lord Hill's coming and Sir Hugh Greene's going may have resulted in no administrative instruction to change anything, but if one examines a cross-section of the statements made by various individuals associated with the BBC in the years from 1968 to 1971, the evidence of a new current of thought is indisputable.

Hardly had the satire shows run their course when in April 1968—nine months after Lord Hill's arrival at the Corporation —the late Tom Sloan, head of BBC light entertainment, thought it necessary to ask his producers to cut out jokes about Prime Minister Harold Wilson.

'It was a purely personal decision on my part,' he told a *Sunday Express* reporter. 'There was a rash of jokes about Mr Wilson, and after sitting through four shows in a row containing them, I simply got bored.

'I told my producers: "Don't do it." The jokes are frequently repetitious, and they are simply not funny any more. Primarily it was nothing to do with Mr Wilson. I would have done the same thing if there had been a rash of jokes about Mr Heath.'

Certainly one man's boredom is another man's giggle. What may have irritated Mr Sloan having sat through four shows in a row need not necessarily have irritated viewers. Were the jokes really so bad as to warrant such an over-all edict?

For example, would Mr Sloan have disapproved of The Wilson Credibility Test which was heard on *The Eleventh Hour?* 'If he strokes his chin, he is telling the truth,' said the commentator, using a series of still pictures of Mr Wilson to illustrate the words. 'If he blinks his eyes, he is telling the truth. If his lips are moving, he is lying.'

Or how would he have rated John Bird's joke on *Once More With Felix?* 'I was walking along a canal and saw Harold Wilson struggling in the water,' said Mr Bird. ' "Help! Help!

Save me!" shouted the Prime Minister. I looked at him floundering in the canal and said to myself, "I wonder what he's really thinking," and went home.'

In attributing deceit and deviousness to politicians both these jokes follow a long and honourable comic tradition. No one expects such remarks to be taken literally. When they refer to a particular individual, such as a Prime Minister, they will only succeed if they reflect a prevailing attitude and a opinion shared by audience and comic. If the joke does not light up some accepted truth it will fall flat, and no one will laugh. For a comedian that is the ultimate penalty. Since Tom Sloan was one of the primary begetters and strongest supporters of those outrageous comedy shows *Steptoe and Son* and *Till Death Us Do Part*, it cannot be said that his record as an executive shows timidity. But those shows were in tune with the more daring, more liberated phase of Greene's era. The edict to stop jokes about Harold Wilson was in tune with the more conventional, less controversial atmosphere that returned towards the end of Greene's reign. The ban on Wilson jokes could not, of course, last long. But jokes about politicians have since that casual edict been generally more amiable and less cruel than in the days of the ruthless satire shows.

Other evidence that things were changing at the BBC had come a few months before the official disapproval of Wilson jokes. In February 1968 *Till Death Us Do Part* ended without any indication that another series was planned for the future. Since this was, as we have seen, the most popular comedy show in BBC history, it appeared more than odd that it should be abandoned. Normally a successful show of this kind would be brought back year after year until the ratings indicated that the public was finally sick of it. Yet after only two seasons—and at the height of its popularity—it was coming to an end. Naturally one had to ask whether Alf Garnett, its vulgar, working-class hero, was pushed off the BBC or whether he died a natural death? According to Johnny Speight, creator and writer of the series, Alf Garnett was smothered by an artistic climate in which he could not survive.*

'We have been irritated by a number of idiotic and unreasonable cuts,' he said. 'The trouble has been since Lord Hill's arrival at the BBC and I could be the victim of new policies. I would write another series for the BBC but only if this censorship was stopped.'

* The series did return in September 1972, but its audacity now seemed old-fashioned and routine.

Symptomatic of the continuing shift towards traditional respectability was the appointment of Shaun Sutton, as the new head of BBC Drama. It was not so much Mr Sutton's credentials—he was eminently qualified for the job since he had been head of serials and responsible in his time for programmes like *Softly, Softly, Dr Who*, and *The Forsyte Saga*—but the statements he made when he took over his post that indicated his suitability for promotion in the Hill hierarchy. NEW TV CHIEF HATES VIOLENCE AND SWEARING was the headline in *The Guardian* story. DRAMA HEAD'S CAUTIOUS LINE ON VIOLENCE was the headline in *The Times* announcing the appointment on 9 May 1969.

In the interviews he gave, Mr Sutton supported a continuing policy of experiment and controversy in BBC Drama, but even more did he emphasize the necessity of doing such things with discretion and good taste.

'Where sex and violence become ugly and unnecessary,' he told Olga Franklin of the *Daily Mail*, 'then I think it is bad writing. Where it offends people's ordinary taste, then no matter how modern, it is bad writing.

'You can go down some very dark alleys if you do it with taste and responsibility. It is marvellous what you can do by closing the book at the right moment. Or closing the bedroom door if you like. It can be much more effective.'[3]

In sentiment and tone they echoed perfectly the concepts laid down by that wishy-washy encyclical, *Broadcasting and the Public Mood*. Freedom for the artist within the bounds of good taste; liberty to tackle themes of corruption and decadence so long as it is discreet and not unduly shocking. But taken literally it is a formula that would deny to television the work of some of the most significant and important playwrights in the contemporary theatre. The deliberate display of bad taste in an effort to undermine the hypocrisy of good taste, the overt use of pornography and violence to illuminate the superficiality and cruelty of some traditional values, are exactly the technical devices used by a good many post-war dramatists.

Mr Sutton's objections might have denied to the BBC some of the best works of writers like John Osborne, Harold Pinter, Edward Bond, Tennessee Williams, David Mercer—not to mention practically the entire range of the young avant-garde theatre.

This drift towards more popular programming and the retreat from controversy was the result of the now ascendant view that the Corporation had gone too far under Greene. What the

BBC wanted now was a Director General who could be trusted to hold the tiller firm in this less troublesome direction. When Charles Curran was appointed to take over from Sir Hugh in March 1959, the BBC got just the man. Like Sir Hugh, the forty-seven-year-old Curran was a BBC professional. After graduating from Cambridge, and after four years with the Indian Army, he joined the BBC as a talks-producer in 1947. Except for a short spell of two years out of the BBC as Assistant Editor of *Fishing News*, a trawling magazine, Curran's entire adult career has been associated with radio. He was head of External Broadcasts and then Secretary of the Corporation.

An Irish Roman Catholic—he was born in Dublin but brought up in Yorkshire—Curran is a tall, articulate man with a notoriously short temper and a manner of dismissing in conversation views he does not share with brusque, even rude, decisiveness. Although fond of music, a good linguist, and a wine connoisseur, he listed 'refereeing coarse Rugby' as his only recreation in *Who's Who*. Here was a purposeful administrator who could be relied upon to restrain any intellectual or political excesses of his staff and whose liberal threshold would be narrower than that of his predecessor. To suggest, as some newspapers did, that he was chosen to play poodle to Lord Hill's mastiff was a complete misreading of the man. His bark and his bite were strictly his own. They just happened to come from approved kennels recognized by Lord Hill and the BBC Governors.

Charles Curran has always insisted that he was in complete accord with what Sir Hugh Greene had been doing at the BBC and that his period of office would attempt to be a continuum of his philosophy and policies. Yet, in spite of his protests, one senses his reservations about Greene's approach, an undue emphasis on balance and consensus responsibility, a justification of the BBC's entertainment function, which have helped to still those turbulent elements that gave the Corporation its few years of stimulating notoriety.

Only a few days after he took office, Mr Curran told Nicholas de Jongh of *The Guardian* that Hugh Greene's ideal was the extension of freedom. 'The chance was there to extend it,' he said. 'All we have to do is to emulate him. There isn't any better ideal.'

Fair enough. Then come the buts, the buts which are the spirit of *Broadcasting And The Public Mood* and which always manage to negate the brave and liberal phrases that precede them. 'But,' continued Mr Curran to *The Guardian*, 'within that ideal, I think of C. P. Scott's remark: "Comment is justly subject to a self-imposed restraint. It is well to be frank. It is even better to be fair." [4]

Another clue to Curran's broadcasting philosophy and his programme priorities was contained in an interview he gave to *Campaign* magazine. 'I think there's a danger of boring people with public affairs,' he said. 'In terms of proportions of time, entertainment of different kinds must obviously be the first consideration in all radio and television. I think you can very easily get to the point where people turn you off because you're dealing with things which don't entertain them, in any continuous sense, and I think current affairs can very easily get into that position.'

Such sentiments may, in a sense, be truisms. Any realist knows that in any foreseeable television service in Britain more hours will be devoted to entertainment than to anything else. But it is the apologetic note about current affairs programmes and the ready statement that 'entertainment must obviously be the first consideration' which starkly contrasts with the way in which Sir Hugh Greene would have discussed the same issue.

Doubts about the BBC's current policies manifested themselves in a remarkable outburst of public protest about the Corporation's plans for radio in the 1970s. Since this book is concerned with television and not radio, it is not my intention to describe in any detail the arguments that raged for almost a year over this subject. But it is necessary to skim through an outline of the controversy to show the uncertainties and suspicions that had arisen in certain cultural, academic, and broadcasting quarters about the direction the BBC was taking and the policies it was pursuing.

The basic aims of the changes in the Corporation's radio structure were to cut costs, to divert minority programmes into a planning scheme that would get them more listeners, and to change the Reithian concept of 'mixed' programmes within a channel into a more rigid division of subject matter. Using a cost-effectiveness yardstick, it was soon clear that the Third Programme—innovated by Sir William Haley and a truly remarkable achievement of experimental, cultural, and often elitist broadcasting—was the most costly and uneconomic feature of radio.

The BBC's plan for correcting this economic imbalance and justifying the cost of minority programmes was contained in the document *Broadcasting in the Seventies*, issued in July 1969. It recommended the complete ditching of mixed programming on a single channel—i.e. news, documentaries, music, sport, light entertainment appealing to all interests and all 'brow' levels—and substituting four rigidly specialized networks, each catering for a different area of broadcasting. Radio 1 would have pop music. Radio 2 would have light music. ('To their respective fans, Emperor Rosko and Eric Robinson barely inhabit the same planet let alone the same air waves,' read the document.) Radio 3 would be confined to classical music and a few selected serious documentaries and plays. Radio 4 would be occupied with the spoken word—panel games, series, current affairs, plays, documentaries. The document also contained new plans for local radio, regional broadcasting, and the disbandment of some orchestras.

Suspicions about what the BBC was up to and what it would do to minority programmes had been aroused by a leak in the press, a few weeks before the Corporation's plans were made public, about the disbandment of four important orchestras. They were the Scottish Symphony, the Northern Dance, the London Studio Players, and the Training Orchestra. Other regional orchestras were also threatened. Over three hundred orchestral musicians would lose their jobs if all the plans were implemented.

There was such a violent eruption of protest from artists, led by Yehudi Menuhin, from newspapers and MPs that the Postmaster General, John Stonehouse, had to step in and ask the BBC to reconsider its plans. When, a few weeks later, on 14 August 1969, Mr Stonehouse announced an increased licence fee of ten shillings—a combined TV-radio licence of £6 10s—he was able to tell the Commons that the BBC had agreed not to go ahead with their proposal to disband the orchestras. Whatever else the BBC plans and the reaction against them had done, they certainly made the Government move fast to give the Corporation some of the extra revenue for which it had been clamouring.

The row over the orchestras was only a foretaste of what was to come. Anger was provoked not only by the proposals made in the BBC's paper on broadcasting, but by the apparent secrecy in which such important decisions were made. The decision to abandon the special and elitist aspect of the Third Programme—where such esoteric delights as an anthology of *poèsie sonore*, organ music of sixteenth-century Portuguese composers, Jarry's *Ubu Enchained*, and talks on Darwin could be had—was particularly distressing to the professors and artists who wrote angry letters to *The Times* and joined pressure groups like The Campaign for Better Broadcasting, formed in September 1969, in an effort to deter the BBC from its act of cultural vandalism.

The entire artistic Establishment of the country seemed at one time engaged in signing petitions or letters about the BBC. The Poet Laureate, Cecil Day Lewis; Professor Hugh Trevor-Roper, Sir Michael Redgrave, Professor Nevill Coghill, Sir Basil Liddle Hart, Sir Isaiah Berlin, Dr Alan Bullock, Vice-Chancellor of Oxford University; Lord Franks, E. M. Forster; forty dons from King's College, Cambridge; Sir John Gielgud, Dame Peggy Ashcroft, Sir Bernard Lovell, Bertrand Russell, and Harold Pinter were among the worthies who joined in the fray.

Pleading a misunderstanding of their intentions and urging the protestors to give the new framework a chance, BBC executives in counter-letters and interviews tried to assuage their critics. They were reassured in their stance by quite clear evidence that the public at large could work up no interest in the matter. 'Despite all the public argument,' wrote Ian Trethowan, the new managing director of BBC radio, 'we have received fewer than 1,000 letters from ordinary listeners since *Broadcasting in the Seventies* was issued—far fewer, for instance, than when we took off the Dales.'[5] This implication that the whole affair was but a storm in a High Table teacup, and that it reflected no significant section of public opinion in the land, merely roused the opposition to greater and louder efforts.

'Details aside, the nub of the matter is this,' said a leader in the *Times Literary Supplement* on 25 December 1969, 'the BBC now believes that the public should be given what it wants; its critics believe that it is the responsibility and privilege of the BBC to choose what is good to be given. Clearly the two positions overlap to a certain extent, but the BBC defines its own position with an emphasis quite foreign to that of Lord Reith and the Pilkington Committee. . . . The BBC seems to be quite clear in its mind that the only product it is interested in supplying is one that people need, or think they need. It is voluntarily submitting itself to that slavery to audience ratings, surveys, etc., from which it can and ought to be free. . . . The public entertains only vague notions about what they want from their radio, television and newspapers, and it is the BBC's job—and it should be its mandate—to lead, to create a taste for what it believes to be worth having not to attempt to satisfy a hypothetical public taste.'

And in the same leader, the art critic Bryan Robertson was quoted with approval. He thought that the BBC had been the greatest educative force of the twentieth century. 'Millions of people have been educated by the BBC. The BBC should not act as a patron, but as a pace-maker, as a creator. The issue at stake is the issue of a failure of nerve, and a breakdown in imagination.'

Further evidence of the growing seriousness of the rot in confidence was an unprecedented act of rebellion on the part of one hundred and thirty-four programme planners and producers of the BBC. In breach of their contracts not to communicate directly with the press, they signed a letter to *The Times*, published on 14 February 1970, objecting to the changes.

'The many professional signatories from within the BBC to recent letters emphasizes, as nothing else has yet done, the extent of an upheaval without precedent in the Corporation,' wrote Sir Robert Lusty to *The Times* on 8 February 1970. '. . . The present discontents go deeper than a concern about new plans for radio. One needs no access to inside information to know this. No amount of explanation, compromise, rhetoric or plain arrogance can continue to conceal the fact that something somewhere has gone seriously wrong with the BBC. How much derives from the new conceptions of Lord Hill of the functions of its chairman; how much from the oddities and hasty adoptions of the McKinsey recommendations; how much from real financial stringency; how much from any governmental intention to force a change of character; how much from a failure to explain (let alone convince) it is hard to say, and we are not told. . . .'

Such a cry of alarm from the man who had been Acting Chairman of the BBC in the brief period between Lord Normanbrook's death and Lord Hill's arrival could not go unheeded. On 21 February the Board of Governors of the BBC signed a letter to the same newspaper expressing their complete agreement with the new radio plans and their absolute confidence in both Lord Hill and the Director General. The day before the significant voice that had so far been absent from this controversy made itself heard. In a letter of chastising severity, Sir Hugh Greene, now one of the BBC Governors instead of its Director General, roundly attacked the critics of the BBC's radio plans.

Except for some desultory protests which rumbled on and a rather muddled debate in the House of Lords on 25 February, which, on the whole, pooh-poohed the fears of the dissidents, the Great Radio Row was over. The plans implemented in April 1970 had perhaps marginally reduced on Radio 3 the more extreme esoteric leanings of its predecessor, but only the most demanding disciples of the Third Programme could truly say that they had been seriously deprived. For example, a year after the new system had been implemented you could still hear on the first Sunday in April 1971 a schedule which included music by Beethoven, Schoenberg, Haydn, and Rachmaninov; *Prometheus Bound*, derived from Aeschylus and written by Robert Lowell; a dramatization of *The Morte D'arthur*; a study of Arbeau's 'Orchesographie'; and the music of sixteenth-century dances. Hardly a philistine's delight.

Strangely enough, during this long and passionate debate about the future of radio hardly any concern at all was expressed about television. If one studies the names of those most fiercely involved, one can venture an explanation about this curious disinterest in the small screen. Most of the protagonists were middle-aged dons, intellectuals, and artists with a romantic and nostalgic attachment to Reithian radio. Television, on the other hand, never personally involved them. They did not know it in their youth. They rarely appeared on it because what they had to offer was seldom wanted on an entertainment-oriented medium. They did not look at it very much. They treated it, as did most middle-aged and elderly politicians, with a mixture of tolerance and contempt. Therefore, although they could whip themselves up into a public-spirited frenzy about radio, they could generate no real interest in the social consequences of television. On 20 February 1970, I wrote the following letter to *The Times* which was published on the same day as Sir Hugh Green's letter denouncing the BBC rebels and critics.

> In the past few weeks your correspondence columns have echoed the concern of a wide section of the population about the prospect of a deterioration in the quality of BBC radio if present plans are implemented. Letters have been written by groups of distinguished professors, writers, artists, musicians, journalists and broadcasters. While appreciating and supporting their fears, I cannot understand why there has been no similar concern expressed about the continuous and relentless deterioration in the quality of BBC television.
>
> By any assessment, the impact of television upon the morals, values and vision of the British people is far more

persuasive, powerful and significant than that of radio. By any yardstick, the quality of programmes on BBC-1 is far less responsible and mature than the general level of BBC radio. No matter how low radio sinks, it will still have a long way to go to reach the depressing standards accepted as normal on BBC-1 television.

Is it accepted, then, by so many responsible and distinguished people that television is now beyond cure or redemption and that their protests could do nothing to reverse the downward plunge of BBC television standards, with all the potential damage to our society that such a deterioration would inevitably entail?

Needless to say, the rest was silence. Not a single letter, either supporting or rebutting this assessment, was subsequently printed in *The Times* on the question of television standards or their social significance.

Although the furore over radio had had no direct effect on BBC television programmes, it had roused suspicions which the Corporation was going to have difficulty in placating. These arguments and protests coincided with the crisis of commercial television—the failure of the new companies to live up to their promises, and the wholesale exodus of executives from London Weekend Television, as related in a previous chapter. The broadcasting media became the focus of noisy debate and controversy. New pressure groups were formed to keep a watchful eye upon the activities of the television hierarchy. There was the 76 Group, composed of producers, writers, and junior executives, representing both the BBC and the commercial companies, who were determined to make the views of those working in broadcasting known to their bosses and politicians. The Free Communications Group, a more politically motivated organization, campaigned for social ownership of the means of communication. Its publication, *The Open Secret*, had been the first to reproduce in detail the confidential applications of the new companies for franchises in 1968.

Thus in less than five years there had been proliferation of pressure groups determined to keep under keen surveillance the activities of the broadcasting authorities. The National Viewers' and Listeners' Association, the 76 Group, the Campaign for Better Broadcasting, the Free Communications Group, TRACK, Cosmo had only one thing in common—their respect for the power of broadcasting and their suspicions that that power might not be exercised correctly. No other medium—the press, cinema, theatre, publishing—had ever had to contend with such incessant outside criticism and surveillance. In itself it was a measure of the anxiety—not shared by legislators or broadcasters—felt by a large number of people about the influence that broadcasting, and particularly television, was having on British society. It should also be said that although these groups were busy and noisy they were always a decided minority. They did not represent the views of the general public or the Establishment, who thought and cared little about television's social consequences.

But while traumatic convulsions were taking place in the press about the possible changes in the content of radio, a much more subtle change was taking place in BBC television. Without any policy statements or directives or instructions, the provocative structure of the Greene regime was being slowly dismantled. Nothing overt was readily discernible, but the mood was less receptive to protest and dissent and more amenable to consensus thinking and reflecting the status quo.

'I tend to see the Corporation at the moment as the equivalent of an old-established restaurant which has taken over a great eating-house chain,' said critic George Melly in *The Observer*. 'At first you don't notice the difference: the waiters are the same, the menu identical, but gradually fresh vegetables give way to frozen, the steaks are standardised, and once the fussy old clientele has fallen away, the management rip out the inside and it becomes just another one of their branches.'[6]

Voicing an even blunter view of what was happening to the BBC was Kenneth Eastaugh in the popular tabloid, *The Sun*. 'For me, television in Britain began to go down hill when Lord Hill came on the scene,' said Mr Eastaugh. 'What a pathetic scene it is. There are exceptions, of course. But television, to my mind, is not as entertaining or daring or progressive now as it was before Lord Hill arrived. . . . I believe that the standard of television is dying. And because he is the most powerful man in Television, I'm blaming Lord Hill—for a start.'[7]

Huw Wheldon, BBC TV's Managing Director, had been proclaiming a programme philosophy which in his annual address to the senior staff in April 1970, he had embodied in the words 'pursuit of excellence.' Under this glib phrase almost anything that enjoyed either critical or popular appeal could be justified. *Up Pompeii*, a comedy series relying almost entirely on sexual double entendres, could be as meritorious as an original comedy concept like *Monty Python*; *Match of the Day* could be as significant as Kenneth Clark's *Civilization*. It was an ingenious formula for dressing up anything the public preferred as 'excellent of its kind.' Carried to its logical conclusion it could be argued that 'excellent' whiskey was better for a dipsomaniac than 'cheap' whiskey, that 'excellent' nicotine was less harmful to a chain smoker than 'poor' nicotine. In truth, excellence of this kind created more addicts than the less tasteful stuff. Wrapping up routine and unimaginative entertainment into technically-adept packages merely created a continuing taste for basically meretricious material. It did not raise standards; it merely lowered them or kept them where they were.

In spite of deep misgivings by a growing number of concerned people, the BBC hierarchy insisted that nothing fundamental had changed. Their sensitivity to these criticisms was evident in the number of times senior BBC executives felt themselves compelled to break into print to justify their policies. Nor were their explanations ever particularly convincing.

The argument about BBC policy could not be resolved by listing individual programmes and ticking them off as 'excellent' or 'mediocre,' according to one's private tastes. It was the totality of the BBC's programmes that was at issue—and the way they were distributed throughout the schedules, especially during peak times. What moral, cultural or, aesthetic criteria inspired them?

It seems clear that the criteria for BBC programming was a belief in the primary importance of entertainment. In that same April 1970 speech, Huw Wheldon said he was sick of being 'preached at' by programmes. There were, in his view, basically two sorts of programmes: 'ones that give delight and ones that feature insight'. Recently there had been too much emphasis on 'insight.' In future he looked forward to more programmes that would give 'delight and pleasure.'

In his schedules for BBC-1, there is evidence that Paul Fox was very much in tune with Mr Wheldon's thinking. The senior channel had now accepted as normal the shrinkage of serious programmes at peak time from the 33% proclaimed to Pilkington to a less demanding 22%.

'It is a fact that, in the period 7.00 pm to 10.30 pm, BBC's serious programmes take up, on the average, 22% of those hours,' wrote Mr Fox in *The Listener* of 7 January 1971. Since the article was distributed by the Corporation in a pamphlet called *In The Public Interest: A Six-Part Explanation of BBC Policy*, it is fair to assume that these statistics were viewed favourably by Mr Fox's seniors. What they did not declare is that these figures, as far as BBC-1 was concerned, represented *a drop of one-third* in the number of peak-time serious programmes the BBC claimed was its aim when it testified before the Pilkington Committee and which it proferred as evidence of its public-service character and its difference from its commercial rival.

Inevitably, the existence of BBC-2 must be brought into the statistical equation. Does the high proportion of serious programmes on BBC-2—over 60% during peak times—justify their being cut down on BBC-1? If it could be shown that more and more people are turning to BBC-2 to get the alternative minority or quality programmes they desire then it could reasonably be claimed that the Corporation had not to any important degree reneged on its promises to Pilkington. But though in 1971 there were twenty-five million people with sets capable of receiving BBC-2, there was no sign that there had been a significant drift of viewers to the junior channel. Something like 5% of the potential audience—if we accept JICTAR figures—regularly watched BBC-2. It had ominously and stubbornly remained at this figure for a number of years. Like National Educational Television in America, which attracted about 2% of the nation's viewers, BBC-2 seemed to have acquired a reputation as a cultural ghetto. It was a reputation which would in the end discourage the average viewer from watching it.

In the final analysis, the BBC's claim to the license fee that finances it, to its freedom from advertising revenue, and to its public-service image depends upon the degree to which it offers a different television service to the one provided by the commercial companies. There was no doubt that under Sir Hugh Greene there was a constant, almost aggressive, assertion that such a difference existed and that never could the divergent programming philosophies meet. The BBC's submissions to Pilkington were scathing in their denunciation of the standards of commercial television—it spoke of the 'mental and spiritual poverty' that more commercial television would likely bring about—and were contemptuous of any suggestion of a similarity in the aims, purposes, and methods of the rival services.

In the post-Greene regime, however, the public statements of senior BBC executives do not echo such a concern about charges of 'homogeneity' with the competing channel. Indeed, they view the growing together of the character of the services with a certain degree of equanimity. And when the purposes of broadcasting are discussed, it is remarkable how the phrases that ring from the lips of authoritative spokesmen have in the early 1970s acquired an astonishingly similar tone and emphasis.

Compare, for example, what Greene said about the similarities between ITV and BBC with what his successor, Charles Curran, and the BBC Chairman, Lord Hill, have said on the same subject. In a speech given at the Manchester Luncheon Club in 1960, Greene said:

> I have noticed a tendency in recent pronouncements by some ITA spokesmen to make out that there is no real distinction between the BBC and commercial television as we have it in this country—that commercial television, at any rate here, is a form of public service. Sir Robert Fraser, for instance, when he spoke to this club last May, referred to what he called a 'remarkable homogeneity' between the BBC and ITV: they were in large part, he claimed, 'assimilated'.

> Now, it is no doubt in some ways flattering to us that commercial broadcasting should wish to come in out of the rain under the public-service umbrella; but as the umbrella belongs to the BBC I shall, I hope, be forgiven if I say that there is no room under it for commercial broadcasting. The difference between us and our aims is a real and permanent one.[8]

Now on the same issue listen to Lord Hill:

> Parliament decided on competition between a commercial service and a public service and this has worked well. The qualities, or opposite of qualities, of one tend to rub off on the other. In Independent Television there is a basic respect, an admiration for the BBC with which it is competing.[9]

And Charles Curran:

> I agree that BBC-1 is not very different now from ITV and I do not think this is a bad thing. . . . If you have competition the competitors get more and more like each other. It is absolutely inevitable.[10]

Of course, what is even more important than whether most of BBC television is now like commercial television is whether or not the development, if true, has improved British television as a whole, has raised standards, has stretched and enhanced the medium. Anyone who has read the brief history of British television contained in these pages will find it difficult to discover a tittle of evidence to justify the claim that commercialism has in any significant way changed BBC television for the better. Nevertheless, the myth persists. It was once again given official sanction when Christopher Chataway, Conservative Minister of Posts and Telecommunications, used it to vindicate his plan to bring commercial radio to Britain. In a number of television interviews on 30 March 1971, he trotted out as his major justification for the Government's scheme to set up sixty commercial radio stations, his conviction that BBC television had been improved by the introduction of commercial television.

All objective evidence suggests the opposite. The Pilkington Committee, reporting on six years of commercial television, found that 'the causes of disquiet and dissatisfaction with television are justly attributed very largely to the service of Independent Television.' That takes us to 1961. Seven years later in 1968 Lord Hill found it necessary to cut down no less than three of the fourteen companies—a failure rate of something like 20%. And the recent history of the new franchises and the events at London Weekend are hardly evidence that things have improved very much in the 1970s. How then could such an institution with such a sorry record have managed to improve the quality of BBC television?

Those who argue that the BBC has benefited by competition go back to 1954 and point to the stuffy, staid television service it then transmitted. But the view that what the BBC was doing in 1954 it would still be doing in 1971 were it not for commercial television, is naïve implausible, and impertinent.

What changed the BBC was not the sudden appearance of ITV but the fact that Britain itself was changing and the presence of Sir Hugh Greene as its Director General. Sir Hugh would have been Director General whether commercial television had or had not existed. His determination to sweep away the musty traditions of Reithian orthodoxy and enlarge the range of BBC broadcasting would have been there had commercial television never existed.

The BBC was changed by the young, fresh talents that created the lively, stimulating, controversial television of the 1960s, by those who produced the satire shows, gave current affairs programmes a cutting edge, raised the quality of light entertainment and dared the tricky themes of the *Wednesday Play*. Donald Baverstock, James MacTaggart, Tom Sloan, Ned Sherrin, Kenneth Loach, Tony Garnett, Jack Gold, Johnny Speight, Troy Kennedy Martin, David Mercer, Galton and Simpson, Elwyn Jones, Ken Russell, Giles Cooper, Humphrey Burton, Spike Milligan, Alan Whicker, Derek Hart, Kenneth Allsop, Benny Hill and dozens of others, including Christopher Chataway himself, would have pushed their ideas, energies and talents into the BBC—with or without the challenge of commercial television.

Only in the field of news, and this was more a matter of presentation than content, can it be said that the BBC benefited by the standard set by commercial television. The Independent Television News (ITN) began with a less formal and more casual approach to news reading which the BBC also adopted. But wouldn't such an obvious change have taken place anyway with men like Hugh Greene, Kenneth Adam, Michael Peacock, and Donald Baverstock setting the style and tone of the Corporation? In drama, comedy, variety, serials, satire, documentaries, current affairs, education, art, music, or any other category of television, the BBC owes nothing at all to any inspiration or leadership generated by its commercial rival.

Indeed, it is much more likely that the existence of independent television has discouraged experiment and the expansion of the range of broadcasting because of the BBC's preoccupation with the size of its audiences brought about by commercial competition. The concern about justifying its licence fee, and rivalry aimed not at producing more meaningful programmes but at proving that BBC executives were better at showbiz than the commercial boys have resulted in a deterioration of aim and quality in BBC-1, and a positive retreat from the challenging potential of this significant medium.

Thus in the early 1970's we see a new post-war BBC taking shape. No longer is it inspired by the fierce Reithian principles of Christian values and public-service responsibility. Nor is it any longer motivated by Greene's desire to create an atmosphere of healthy scepticism for the examination of accepted attitudes and views 'which, in many cases, have hitherto been accepted too easily or too long.'[11]

How different are contemporary statements of purpose from the positive creed for broadcasters enunciated by Sir Hugh Greene in a speech made in 1965:

I believe that broadcasters have a duty not to be diverted by arguments in favour of what is, in fact, disguised censorship. I believe we have a duty to take account of the changes in society, to be ahead of public opinion rather than always to wait upon it. I believe that great broadcasting organizations, with their immense powers of patronage for writers and artists, should not neglect to cultivate young writers who may by many be considered 'too advanced,' even 'shocking.'[12]

Compare this declaration of intent with that voiced by Lord Aylestone, Chairman of the Independent Television Authority, in a speech delivered in Leeds in December 1969.

> Television should not be among the pacemakers on public attitudes. . . . It is my view that while we certainly cannot ignore the developments in our sister arts, and while it is certainly our duty to report—in fiction as well as in fact— on changing attitudes, we would be wrong to be among the pacemakers. We would be wrong to be too often, or too far, way-out.[13]

Since Mr Curran feels that is it no bad thing that BBC-1 and ITV are not very different from each other, it is perhaps predictable that his idea of a broadcaster's duty should be so much closer to the spirit of Lord Aylestone's beliefs than to those of Sir Hugh Greene.

A sure way to dampen controversy and discourage concern is to emphasize the entertainment imperative of the television medium. If it is the BBC's primary function to entertain, then it follows that there will be fewer programmes whose main purpose is to inform and educate. And if those that do inform and educate also manage to be entertaining won't that take the heat out of controversial programmes, discourage arguments, and create a jollier atmosphere all round?

So Huw Wheldon told his senior staff that he was sick of being 'preached at' by programmes and was looking forward to more programmes that would give 'delight and pleasure.' So Charles Curran in his Edinburgh speech said that the BBC was out to provide the widest range of what will be enjoyed, and that since what BBC-1 and BBC-2 already offered was so incredibly catholic, a change towards more minority elements would be hard to justify.[14] And so Lord Hill, in his most avuncular style, told an interviewer, 'when the great British public seeks relaxation, say on a Saturday night, there's nothing to be ashamed of in seeking to please the largest number on BBC-1. . . . The majority of the great British public look to television for relaxation. Criticize them for it, if you will, but the fact is undeniable.'[15]

Thus divested of its Reithian passion, and unwilling to carry out the role of a catalyst and stimulant proclaimed by Greene, the BBC looks as if it will be content for the next few years to pirouette at the outer edge of the nation's affairs instead of sharing the heat of its troubled centre. Like its commercial rival and its counterparts in America, whose principal aim is never to be in the vanguard of anything, it will concentrate more and more on the transmission of entertainment and giving the public what the Corporation thinks it wants.

CHAPTER VII

DOES IT MATTER?

And shall we just carelessly allow children to hear any casual tales which may be devised by casual persons, and to receive in their minds ideas for the most part the very opposite of those which we should wish them to have when they are grown-up?—Plato in *The Republic*.

Any debate on broadcasting in the House of Commons or the Lords will have some politician asserting that, with all its faults, British broadcasting is the best in the world. It is a boast that is seldom challenged. Even the American magazine, *Newsweek*, commenting on the BBC's 50th anniversary year and the sudden proliferation of BBC shows such as *Civilization*, *The Forsyte Saga* and *The Six Wives of Henry VIII* on American screens, said that most discriminating American viewers would agree that British television was the best in the world.[1]

Yet few people enquire what 'best' in this context means. Does 'best' mean the television service that attracts most viewers to the box; that makes the most profits for those who supply it; that provides the most entertainment; that most intelligently educates and informs the public; that combines most effectively the functions of education, information, and entertainment; that offers a forum of communication free from state control; that most responsibly propagates or perpetuates the ideological and social values of the state? By each of these individual tests British television is far from the 'best' in the world. American television attracts far more viewers and makes much more money than British TV. Communist régimes as in Russia and China use television far more effectively as an instrument of state education and propaganda. Western Germany, Holland, and Sweden are more conscientious about the social responsibilities of the box and offer a wider range of participation to more elements in society than does British television. And even in the field in which British television now concentrates most of its revenue and talent—entertainment—the average level of its domestic comedy, variety, and action/adventure programmes is well below the technical competence and production values of the networked American show.

Why, then, is British television held in such high esteem by so many people? Aside from the fact that most people who heap such praise upon it rarely study its over-all content but judge its performance on a few isolated high spots, it is probably true that British television has in some ways managed until now to avoid a good many of the excesses that mar television all over the world. It has fought, particularly the BBC, for some measure of independence from Government dictate and control. It has refused to become a mere instrument of state propaganda. It has not succumbed entirely to the entertainment ethos—BBC-2 is retained to act as the cultural conscience of the medium—and the major channels still offer a far larger quota of serious drama, documentaries, and discussion than the major networks in America. Its levels of production and artistic creativity are in general very competent and, on occasions, outstanding. In other words, its greatest virtues are negative ones. It may be that this is the only kind of accomplishment that can be expected of a medium that is still so young and so mysterious in its impact that authority everywhere circumscribes its freedom with suspicion and distrust. The churlish accolade that British television is 'the least worst in the world' is probably a more accurate assessment of its place in universal television. But, some may ask, is that good enough?

These pages have tried to show the haphazard way in which television in Britain has developed. Almost by accident the Reithian concept of public-service broadcasting has been replaced by the view that the prime function of television is to entertain. The competition of commercial TV has forced the BBC to pander to the argument that by 'giving the public what it wants' it is serving the best needs of the nation. The consequences of tempting viewers with frivolity and escapist programmes during peak-time hours on the two major channels is that only small minorities ever see most of the programmes designed to inform and educate, and the large majorities, conditioned to pap, find demanding programmes either indigestible or boring. The consistent record of low viewing figures of BBC-2 reveals how difficult it is to wean the British public to something better or different when its taste has been cultivated to accept and appreciate primarily the trivial.

But can it be seriously argued that this shift away from concerned, committed, and informative television has done the nation any harm? Does it matter how television is used and what it transmits? Is not the ideal function for this electronic toy to act as a relaxant for the tired worker and housewife, as a comforting companion for the elderly and the lonely, as a baby-sitter for the very young, as a diversion to help us to escape from the realities and cares of the day? Is it not, in the last analysis, merely a mirror of the times capable of aggravating nothing, enhancing nothing, creating nothing, destroying nothing that is not already endemic and deep-rooted in the society it is portraying? How can a reflection damage anything?

Was the playwright Keith Waterhouse right when he said: ('TV's power for good or evil is roughly equivalent to that of the hula-hoop'?[2] Or was Malcolm Muggeridge right when he wrote: 'Of all the inventions of our time it is likely to prove the most destructive. Whereas nuclear power can only reduce us and our world to a cinder, the camera grinds us down to spiritual dust so fine that a puff of wind scatters it, leaving nothing behind'?[3]

It is this bewilderment about the real capabilities of television that characterizes the contradictory attitudes that most countries have to it. While everyone from motor car manufacturers to funeral directors will bitterly complain about any alleged misrepresentation of their image or case on the box—presumably because the distortion will have some effect on the viewers—there is astonishingly little concern about the total picture of our society that is transmitted into the homes and conscience of the public most hours of the day and night. While vested interests from politicians to Churchmen will contend that some individual programme, some disfiguring splinter of the mosaic, has adversely affected them, they will display no like anxiety about the impact of the total mosaic upon society as a whole.

We have seen how Harold Wilson fretted over his television image and to what lengths he went to ensure that the medium was amenable and accommodating to politicians. The same obsession with television's ability to affect political fortunes can be seen in America where men like President Nixon and Vice-President Agnew scrutinize and criticize any programme trend they consider adverse to their interests. Yet British and American politicians rarely indicate any interest or concern about television as a socializing force in the state.

Similarly, while the public may occasionally be upset by a four-letter word, a glimpse of nudity, or a particularly horrifying bit of violence, it, too, is content to accept the box as primarily a dispenser of entertainment in the home. In Britain academics and intellectuals who have never been as involved with television as they were with radio—where the cultural standards have always been much higher—also express no serious reservations about the way in which the medium is

structured and oriented. Having to choose between a service influenced by the values of the state or the values of the advertising
man, their instinctive fear of state censorship tends to make them
prefer the less obvious censorship of the market-place.

The equanimity of public, politicians, and intellectuals about
what television might be doing to society is bolstered by the fact
that little serious thinking has been done on the subject and
there are few reliable research findings to guide one. Although
there has been almost a plethora of research into television's
impact on politics and violence, the more significant issue of
whether the total contents of the box can have significant as
opposed to a minimal influence on society has only been superficially examined.

One of the main reasons for the failure of social scientists to
pinpoint the consequences of television as a whole has been the
unavailability of human beings who have been subjected to it
all their lives. This is because the medium is still so young. It
began to function seriously only in 1947 and is just over twenty-
five years old. Although television is categorized as one of the
most formidable of the mass media, it can only be said to have
deserved such a status when a substantial number of people had
sets in their homes and started to watch them. Strange as it may
seem, the vast majority of people in the world have still never
seen a television set. In 1963 only 5 % of the world's population
had TV sets. In 1972 it is unlikely that much more than 10 % of
peoples have TV.

To discover, then, a substantial body of persons who could be
said to have been conditioned by the box—raised, as it were, on
an electronic nipple—one would be forced to confine's one's
research to only three countries—Britain, America, and Canada.
If we assume that television can only be justly called a mass
medium when it is being watched by at least 50 % of the homes
in the country in which it is operating, then these three countries
alone have as yet spawned a telly generation. The relevant
dates are these: America had 50 % ownership in 1953, Canada
in 1955, and Britain in 1956. Expansion of TV ownership after
these dates was rapid and enormous. By the early 1960s these
three countries could be classified as total TV societies because
more than 90 % of homes possessed sets. They alone were
graced—or bedevilled—by a majority of children who had
watched television almost from the time they could first walk
and talk and carried that conditioning experience with them
through adolescence into maturity.

Thus in 1972 the first telly generation in America consists of over half the people between the ages twenty and twenty-four. They began watching the box from the age of two to five. In Britain and Canada that generation is a few years younger— seventeen to twenty-one. It must be remembered that by 1972 not a single person in the world over twenty-five had had his early formative years influenced by television. In Britain, Canada, and America, however, almost every child under the age of ten and the majority of those under twenty-one have been reared in a TV home. The Jesuits claimed that if they had a child until he was seven, they would have the man for the rest of his life. The behaviourial sociologists strongly support the dominating influence of environment upon the shaping of attitudes and personality. What, then, is television likely to do to a society where everyone is a telly child almost from birth? Have these three national TV generations anything in common that might give us a clue?

In due course, some time in the mid-1970s, other countries like Australia, West Germany, Sweden and Japan will also find themselves with a generation the majority of whom have reached maturity in close contact with the box. The way television will have affected them will obviously depend upon the kind of television to which they have been subjected. Although we owe a great deal to Marshall McLuhan for alerting us to the fundamental manner in which various media affect our lives, his view that the contents of the medium are irrelevant seems not only unproveable but perverse. It is challenged, for example, by that other much-discussed thinker of our times, Herbert Marcuse, who considers that television in America indoctrinates and manipulates people to accept the virtues of affluence and the profit motive through entertainment and commercials. It thus positively obscures and disguises the contradictions of capitalism and reinforces the system. One does not have to agree with Marcuse's thesis to accept his view that the contents of television are significant in shaping the attitudes of a society. Can it really be argued, for example, that Britain would be exactly the same today if Reithian concepts of broadcasting had prevailed instead of the ones that have taken its place? This is not to say that Britain would have been better or worse; but it certainly would have been different. Marginally different or significantly different? That is the unanswered question.

By a strange coincidence the three countries that were the first to produce a telly generation—more than half of the generation reared on the box from their earliest years—have a similar philosophical approach to television's function in society.

Although there is a pious hope firmly embedded in legislation and governmental pronouncements that the medium shares the triple obligation of informing, educating, and entertaining, in practice television in Britain, America, and Canada is primarily an entertainment medium with the supplementary purpose of selling goods. When most people are viewing—at peak times between 6.30 pm and 10 pm—the predominant diet of programmes is made up of light entertainment and sport. In America 95 % of peak-time shows are devoted to entertainment. In Canada 85 % of prime time is entertainment. In Britain the commercial channel transmits about 90 % peak-time escapist and undemanding programmes while BBC-1 has a 78 % peak-time ration of light entertainment and sport.

As we have already seen, attempts to get mass audiences that have been weaned on pap to enjoy something meatier have not been very successful in Britain, where BBC-2 rarely manages to win more than 5 % of the nation's viewers. In America, where the Public Service Broadcasting network attempts to fulfil the task of seriously informing and educating viewers, the ratings are even more disheartening with little more than 2 % of the potential audience willing to tear themselves away from the diversions offered by the popular networks.

Undoubtedly the most singular aspect of television as either an art form or a medium is the compulsive quality of its appeal. It is more a habit than a medium. Once hooked, the television addict will watch almost anything. In most homes in Britain and America the set is switched on almost as regularly and routinely as the electric light. In Britain the number of sets switched on every evening of the year remains constant within one or two percentage points. The public prefers light to serious programmes, but if there are no light programmes to watch— when, for example, all three channels in Britain are occupied with a Party Political Broadcast—the total amount of viewers who turn the picture off is marginal.

Both the very young and the very old constitute the largest sectors of heavy viewers. In America the average viewing figure for children is 4 to $4\frac{1}{2}$ hours per day. Since this is an average figure many children obviously spend more hours in front of the small screen. Amongst the poor and uneducated, children spend an average of 5 to 6 hours a day watching the box. One American statistic testified to the fact that in some slum areas of New York, children between the ages of three and five looked at television 8 to 10 hours a day.

In Britain children view less, probably only because until

very recently round-the-clock television as in America has not been available to them. The average British home has its set switched on about 5 hours per day and the child watches it on average about 3 to 3½ hours per day. With the advent of morning and afternoon television, these figures are bound to rise. It has been calculated that by the time the average American child has graduated from his secondary or high school, he will have spent 10,800 hours in school and more than 20,000 hours watching television. It is likely that this figure will soon be matched in Britain.

The environmental factors that educationalists and sociologists generally accept as the most important in a child's life are his home and parents, his neighbourhood, his school, and his church. In totalitarian societies, the ideological factor replaces the religious one. Yet in television societies none of these important factors absorb and occupy more of a child's waking hours than does the small screen. Few children listen to their parents, their teachers, their priests for four hours a day with the concentration and involvement they give to the box. Perhaps only with their own age groups, their peer groups, do children share a similar amount of hours of social togetherness. And their peer groups, being similarly conditioned by television, reciprocate and reinforce the ideas and values that they absorb from the electronic pictures in their living rooms.

It is obvious, then, that television must be counted as a fifth factor—joining home, school, neighbourhood, and church—as one of the significant socializing influences in a child's life. And just as any society would be concerned about the quality of home, school, neighbourhood, religious instruction that affected its children, so ought any responsible society care about the quality of television that is beamed at the telly generations.

The conversion of British television from that of a benign headmaster to a familiar clown only matters if society is adversely affected by such a change. If old ladies get pleasure out of undemanding programmes, if tired workers and weary housewives can escape from their cares watching comedy shows or sport, if children can be kept quiet by TV's delights, what on earth is wrong with a broadcasting service that considers entertainment, rather than education or information, its top priority?

But if in the process of providing frivolous and trivial entertainment, television also convinces a large number of those brought up on its message that life, too, is frivolous and trivial, would society be ready to pay such a price for its ration of fun and games in the evening? Suppose that because the young believed television truly reflected the society they lived in, was truly a mirror of what the future held for them, might not some of them become revolted by the silly, greedy, purposeless image of life the box beams at them almost 85 % of the time that most of them are watching it? And if they were revolted by such a life style which their parents apparently admired and cherished, might they not react to the prospect of existing in such a cultural wasteland by either moving violently against it or opting out of it altogether? And if amongst the three countries that raised their first telly generation on entertainment-oriented pro-grammes, there was a remarkable coincidental rise in violence, contempt for authority, drug-taking, rejection of social values— all symptoms of either revolt or resignation from social norms —not shared by the non-telly generations nor experienced in countries that had a different TV philosophy, might it not be about time to enquire seriously into the possibility that Govern-ments and the Establishment are dangerously mishandling this important and powerful fifth factor in our children's lives?

In my book *The Ravenous Eye*, I have examined in some detail the evidence that television might be a serious contributor to the manifestations of violence, rejection of authority, widening generation gap, unprecedented drug-taking as a gesture of defiance and escape from straight society, that markedly dis-tinguished the telly generations in Britain, Canada, and America from their counterparts in other countries. It is possible in this concluding chapter only to skim through the argument in order to substantiate the view that British television has taken a wrong turning in making the provision of entertainment its prime function.[4]

Since it is readily acknowledged that television is the most effective selling medium man has yet devised—American advertisers lavish close to three billion dollars upon it annually— its persuasive powers must also be effective in other areas of human behaviour. Politicians, for example, have no doubts about its influence upon voting patterns. Any vested interest that feels itself maligned on a television programme—the Church, the motor car industry, the film business have all recently complained bitterly about the contents of individual programmes—is convinced of the potent impact of the box on their fortunes. Why, then, should it be assumed that the total mosaic of the box, its total contents, has no significant influence on society—particularly the young—and why has there been so little effort made to examine the social consequence of the whole of television rather than merely its isolated fragments or splinters?

When we convert the box into an entertainment dispenser is it possible that, like Pandora, we might be surprised to discover how many evils are let loose when its contents are released? If a substantial proportion of programmes, for example, depict violence as normal, acceptable, and even moral, why should not that message be as persuasive as commercials successfully selling the aphrodisiacal powers of armpit deodorants? Entertainment television as it has been organized in Britain, America, and Canada relies for a large measure of its contents upon programmes in which overt or concealed violence is a major ingredient of their appeal. Is it possible, then, that one of the loudest messages of the box—that violence is normal and merely mirrors life—has gone unheard when other messages of the box concerning goods, politicians, relgion, industry, and trade unions constantly make an impact which society recognizes and acknowledges? Because violence-oriented programmes are so much a routine aspect of the totality of entertainment television, it is necessary to examine the impact they have made on the first telly generation. If this staple diet of British and American schedules has had little or no influence upon them, then it could be reasonably argued that other environmental factors have successfully counteracted and nullified any negative effects of this type of television. But if this generation has got the message and adopts attitudes to violence consistent with the ethical criteria of the small screen, the chances are that it is also being affected by other hidden messages that seep through the interstices of the mosaic. Let us look, then, briefly at the argument that increased violence and entertainment-biased television are related.*

In America over the last twenty years there have been almost a dozen Governmental investigations into the connection between violence and television. The earliest enquiries tended either to pooh-pooh any such link or to confess there was neither the methodology nor the evidence to warrant any conclusive judgment. But with the passage of time and the accumulation of long-term evidence, there are now few serious broadcasters or social scientists left who would stoutly maintain that there is no causal relationship between violence and the box. The last-ditch defenders of the right to saturate shows with violent incidents still argue that such programmes have a cathartic effect

---

* A much fuller examination of television and violence is to be found in the chapter 'Cain's Kindergarten' in my book, *The Ravenous Eye*.

which drains off violence or at worst only affects the socially disturbed and abnormal elements in the population. Both President Johnson's Commission on Violence in 1969 and the U.S. Surgeon General's Report in 1972 have decisively squashed and rejected such arguments. President Johnson's Committee said that the vast majority of experimental studies did not support the catharsis theory and found that observed violence *stimulated* aggressive behaviour rather than the reverse. The Surgeon General's report has produced convincing evidence that TV violence affects normal children as well as abnormal ones.

To understand these findings by these two distinguished bodies of lawyers, social scientists, politicians, it is necessary only to consider some of the factual evidence that was presented to them. President Johnson's Commission calculated that from 1964 to 1968 between one-half and two-thirds of all programmes in the 7 to 10 pm prime-time slot were of the action and adventure type containing some degree of violence. Between 4 and 6 pm, when a large proportion of children were watching, this ration of violence-oriented programmes was even higher.

This means that the American child who spends on average 4 hours a day watching the box, half of his viewing being concentrated on programmes with violent themes and actions, will be spending almost 15 hours a week in a violence-saturated environment. It can be safely calculated that the bulk of teenagers in America in 1972 had spent one-sixth of their waking hours absorbed in the fictionalized violence of television. If there is added to this dose of violent imagery, the average quota of mayhem, cruelty, and murder he received from reading comic books, crime and adventure magazines, and films, it is possible to estimate that an American youngster had been immersed from between one-quarter to one-fifth of his waking hours in some form of dramatic or vicarious violence.

Similar statistics apply to Canada, and the British figures are not much less. Leicester University's Centre for Mass Communication Research, investigating a typical week in April 1972 found that 62% of all programmes on BBC and ITV contained violence, and that there were more violent incidents during the peak viewing time for schoolchildren—i.e. up to 9 pm—than there were after they had gone to bed. A BBC Audience Research Department survey studying 1,558 programmes transmitted on all channels between November 1970 and May 1971 found that 63% of all dramatic fiction shown on TV contained some violence, that there was no substantial difference between BBC and commercial TV levels of violence, that children's TV contained more violence than adult TV, that British TV showed more killings than American TV, and that American programmes were more violent—with less killing—than British TV programmes.

The survey also compared peak-time viewing in America and Britain and found that 'whereas 84% of U.S. networked prime-time entertainment programmes in 1969 contained some violence, only 58% of the comparable British programmes in 1970/71 included any major incidents.' It is interesting to note the use of the word 'only' in this context. Such a comparative statistic may be reassuring to the BBC Research Department but I doubt if it will console anyone else.[5]

It can be estimated that the ordinary British and American child will witness on television something between 20 to 30 minor or major violent incidents per day—a rate of between 5 to 9 violent happenings per hour. Some argue that this ration of violence is acceptable because it merely reflects every-day life and that the box is merely holding up a mirror to society. But how true is this bizarre compendium of violence to reality? President Johnson's Attorney General, Ramsey Clark, has calculated that in 1967 an individual's chance of being a victim of violence in America was 1 in 400 during the year.[6] On a daily basis, the odds of his coming into contact with violence was 1 in 146,000. But on TV the American child comes into contact with violence—beatings, garrotting, asphyxiations, knifings, death-ray obliteration—something like 25 times a day. Thus the vision of violence an American child gets from the small screen is exaggerated by something like 4,000,000 times over the violence he is likely to experience in his domestic activities. In Britain the gap between telly life and real life is of the same sort of exaggerated dimension. By what stretch of the imagination or extension of dramatic license can such gargantuan distortions be defended on the grounds that they are merely mirroring what life is really like?

It is clear then that of all the attributes of the human spirit—wisdom, curiosity, logic, charity, pity, greed, compassion, to name but a few—violence is by far the greatest pre-occupation of entertainment-dominated television. In its various manifestations violence fills more hours of the box at peak times than the combined total of every other quality of man's wide and ranging personality. Obviously we must ask ourselves what does this type of TV say about violence. Does it consistently condemn it or consistently excuse it? Does it encourage it or discourage it? Does it generate emulation or provoke rejection of violence?

A study group at the University of Pennsylvania submitted evidence to President Johnson's Commission on Violence of a survey done in 1967 about the attitudes of action-adventure programmes to violence. Most of the series it examined were also seen in Britain. Basing its study upon the activities of leading characters or hero figures whose personalities are usually likely to be admired or emulated by the young, it found that of 455 such leading characters at least half of them inflicted some form of violence upon others. At least one out of every ten was a killer. Police and other official law-enforcement agents were almost as violent as criminals but never paid with their lives. Seven out of every ten official agents of law committed violence, two out of ten with fatal results.

'Being violent or non-violent related most closely to efficiency, emotionality and logic,' says this survey. 'All violents were more efficient, unemotional and logical than all non-violents. Killers were even more efficient and unemotional. And killers who reached a happy ending (mostly heroes) were the most calmly efficient of all.'

Although the conventional attitude to this kind of programme is that its dangers lie in its encouragement to imitative action, the real peril of such programmes is far more subtle. It is true that some elements will be attracted to imitative behaviour by the constant sight of men being mugged, guns being fired, buildings being burned, and aeroplanes being sabotaged. Since some statistics indicate that we have an unstable and psychotic element of almost 20 % amongst the young in countries like Britain and America, even the imitative consequences of such programmes could have serious results. However, it is the message of the mosaic of violence which is far more frightening than its individual sadistic manifestations. This has basically four things to say about violence.

First, violence is usually done by good men for moral and ethical reasons. The hero figure, the man supporting law and justice, wins his case by being better at the karate chop, faster on the draw, more adept at the kick in the groin. The best man is the man who is best at violence.

Second, violence is not very painful nor is it ugly. Blood is rarely seen. Gaping wounds are taboo. Torn bodies are discreetly blacked out. Indians fall painlessly from their horses. Men from space are neatly disintegrated with X-ray guns. The consequences of violence are disguised, hygienized, anaesthetized, diminished.

Third, pity is rarely shown for the victims of violence. It was through pity and terror that we were purged of violence when watching the plays of Euripides and Sophocles. When Agamemnon was murdered or Iphigenia sacrificed it was through the laments of the Chorus and the agonies of the mother or the children that we were roused to consider the dignity of life and the horror of violence. This was what Aristotle meant when he spoke about catharsis. But in television there is no concern for the relatives of the Russian spy who has been garroted by an FBI agent or the children of the gangster who has been dropped to the bottom of the sea in a coffin of cement.

Fourth, society hardly ever demands retribution or a judicial explanation of violence in TV shows. There are no sanctions for killing or mayhem if done by hero characters. Instead of standing trial for murder or manslaughter, the sheriff in *The Virginian* or the police official in *Hawaii Five-O* is usually rewarded after cold-bloodedly killing the bad guys with a smiling blonde and approving fade-out music.

If we couple this message of the desirability of violence in the right hands with the other messages that come out loud and clear from entertainment-oriented television that life is trivial, greedy, silly, then isn't it natural that many minds will grasp the obvious conclusion? If life is cheap and unworthy then is it not both understandable and moral to resort to violence as a means of changing and improving it?

Determined as it is to concentrate most of its energy and attention on the escapist and ephemeral aspects of life, television inevitably has helped condition an entire generation to believe that life is anarchic, disorganized, frivolous, aimless. The total mosaic is not concerned, not serious, not logical, not involved. Into this curious disengaged melange, there are pictured incongrouously the more reflective and responsible aspects of our society—the politicians, the priests, the trade-union leaders, the academics, the doctors, the artists. But in the total TV context, they are but bit players in an electronic show-biz spectacular. Their appearances are minimal, a distraction, an irritation interrupting the delights of *Coronation Street* and *The Andy Williams Show*.

Inevitably these representatives of authority adopt the colourings of their electronic environment. They judge the success of their ideas and standing by their ability to communicate with the public on telly terms. They associate achievement with ratings; they identify progress with popularity. To be 'good on the box' becomes a pre-requisite for reaching the highest summit in politics and public affairs. And to achieve that accolade the serious figures in our society strive to master the techniques of the medium—over-simplification, contentious generalizations, glib dialectic. Cabinet Ministers are ready to present their arguments for entering the Common Market in four minutes flat; bishops are willing to analyse the nature of miracles in three minutes dead; politicians are eager to sell themselves to the electorate, particularly in America, like so many packages of branded goods. Television is not used in a General Election to inform the public about the issues in some forum of national debate. Rather is it used, as it was in the 1970 General Election, as a huckster's Petticoat Lane in which the public had a choice between political detergents, between 'Omo' Wilson and 'Daz' Heath.

Since for many young people the television picture is the only image they have of life outside their own immediate experience, it is not surprising that many of them are disillusioned and dismayed by the world as they have absorbed it in their living rooms. The life style of their elders as it has been reflected on the box—its false values, its relentless triviality, its cavorting establishment—engenders uncertainty, distrust, and contempt. The caricature of the older generation most often seen in the Underground press is that of a middle-aged man clutching a beer can staring glassy-eyed at a television set. This vision of the aimless watching the mindless is something many of the telly generation identify with the societies they want to reject. And their rejection in many cases takes the form of dropping out into hippiedom, seeking alternative visions of existence in drugs, adopting violence as a means of changing a society which they feel they can affect in no other way.

It will, of course, be argued that other media in their time have been blamed for disenchanting the young and encouraging violence. Because the case against comic books, films, novels as significant provokers of violence has not been proved, why should the case against television be taken any more seriously? What has yet not been recognized by those who decry the influence of television is not only the essential differences between media as advanced in the theories of Marshall McLuhan, but the unique manner in which television is experienced.

In the first place, no other media or art form in mankind's history has been absorbed in such massive doses by so many people. How many children look at comic books four hours a day, read novels four hours a day, sit in a cinema four hours a day? Television occupies more hours in a child's life than all other media and art forms put together. It also, in terms of quantity, is the most demanding environmental factor in a child's life. Few children spend as many attentive hours with parents, teachers or priests as they do with the box.

The second difference between television and other media is its visual quality. It appeals to the eye—the most gullible sensory apparatus man has. Instinctively man believes his eyes more than any of his other senses. We acknowledge the homily that seeing is believing. The moving picture gives an illusion of truth and credibility unmatched by any other media. The moving picture also has its peculiar hypnotic quality which is so potent that television is fast replacing cigarettes and alcohol as man's most addictive habit. For those who say what is the difference between television and the moving picture in the cinema, the answer is none, except that the cinema film was never seen as much as the television picture nor was the cinema film seen in the familiar environment of the home. If children born in the 1920s and 1930s had lived in a cinema, slept in a cinema, eaten in a cinema and conducted their domestic lives against a background of moving pictures that not only dealt with the fictional but the actual happenings in society, I doubt if any sociologist or psychologist would contend that such a generation would not be markedly different from the generations that eventually did emerge from those times.

It is this pervasiveness of television, its existence in the most intimate and familiar surroundings of the home, that constitutes television's third major difference from other media. For the young watcher television is not merely moving wallpaper; it is part of the room itself, the home itself, an extension of his personal environment. In other media there is a distinct consciousness of a separation between the individual and the art form or medium he is experiencing. In other media, individuals, particularly the young, are more conscious of their independent control over a medium as well as of a certain detachment from it. A child *picks up* a book or a magazine or a comic strip. He *goes* to the cinema or the theatre. But he *steps into* television. He is surrounded by it, as McLuhan has said, as if it were a warm bath. It is irrevelant to argue that the child can switch the set off. Ask most parents how difficult it is to tear away their child from the box; watch children walking backwards to bed as they try to cling to a glimpse of some preposterous commercial or the beginning of some film they will never see the end of. The box for many of them is not only home, but it is a vision of all of life brought into their home.

Even adults react in a markedly different way to television. I recall seeing on television a man complaining about the rough treatment Harold Wilson, when he was Prime Minister, had received in a *Panorama* interview. 'I did not pay my license fee,' he said, 'so that the Prime Minister could be insulted in my living room.' Had he read that same interview in the *Daily Express*—in his own living room—or watched it in a cinema, he would not have felt that same sense of being personally involved with and intimately touched by the incident.

If, then, we can assume that television's persuasive power as a medium is unique; if we can agree that it has become an environmental factor taking up as much time as such other environmental factors as home, neighbourhood, school, and Church; if we can accept the view that television presents primarily a trivial and escapist version of life when most people are watching it, what concrete evidence is there that this combination of circumstances has had any adverse, or even significant, social consequences in countries like Britain, America, and Canada?

Because an effort has been made to find such evidence in the case of violence, let us see what the facts reveal in that particular social area. If television can be proved to have contributed to a serious rise in violence, surely it is not illogical to assume that it might also have been influential in contributing to such other changes amongst the telly generation such as their intense rejection of orthodox values, their hostility to authority, their search for modes of living which often outrages and shocks their parents, and their involvement in a drug culture. It might be prudent to add at this point that most of the telly generation, of course, are neither rebels, hippies, drug-takers, nor hoodlums. Most of them accept the conventions and goals of their parents and strive to become respectable doctors, lawyers, workers, farmers, and businessmen. But the minority do not. And it is this minority that make up the revolutionary, the criminal, the violent. It is a substantial minority, growing all the time, and their activities have brought anxiety and concern to societies that neither understand them nor have any inkling of what has brought them into being.

In Britain and America the public is concerned about the level of violence today, seemingly greater than it was in the 1920s and 1930s before the advent of television. It may have been more violent in the medieval age or in America's frontier days but a return to the violence of those times would hardly be something any society would view with equanimity. In major cities like New York and Washington doors are bolted almost like bank safes, suburban areas are protected like fortresses with guard dogs and private security police; individuals dare not go out late at night. In Britain the newspapers are filled with accounts of hooliganism at football games, terror in the classrooms, mugging in the streets. For a society that once believed that America's domestic violence could never reach similar proportions in Britian, the British people are no longer so complacent. A survey conducted in 1972 in *The Sun* newspaper found that 62 % of the people felt unsafe when they walked out on their own at night and 90 % could not rest easily when their children went out.

But a most telling proof of how violence has escalated in telly societies lies in a study of the criminal statistics in Britain, America, and Canada. Confining our attention to crimes of violence against the person—assaults, woundings, etc.—it is notable that this particular category of crime has the greatest growth rate of all crimes. Since 1955 was the year when telvision became a mass media in Britain, we can take it as the starting year for analysing any criminal trend that might be related to the box. While the over-all rate of crime from 1955 to 1971 has gone up 300 %, crimes of violence have gone up 600 %. In 1955 there were 7,884 crimes of violence known to the police; in 1971 there were no less than 47,000.

Who committed these crimes? If we take the age group of twenty-one and over—those least likely to have been affected by television—the increase in violent crime in these years has been 450 %. For under seventeens the increase in violent crime has been 900 %; for the age group between seventeen and twenty— the first true telly generation—the increase has been a staggering 1,300 %! In other words, there have been three times as many crimes of violence committed by those brought up on the box as were committed by the generation uninfluenced by it in their formative years.

American statistics show precisely the same trend. Says the FBI's Crime Report of 1969 discussing crimes of violence, 'It is apparent that the involvement of young persons as measured by police arrests is escalating at a pace almost four times their percentage increase in the national population.'

And in Canada? Here again the rate of increase in violent crime has been about 10 % annually—very similar to the increase in Britain and America—with the young being responsible for most of that increase. Says the Canada Year Book of 1970, 'The young men and women in the age group between 16–24 account for 22 % of the total population 16 years and over, but they form half of the criminal population committing indictable offences.'

Now what is curious about this similar crime profile in three Western telly societies is that it is confined almost exclusively to these countries. The phenomenal leap in crimes of violence amongst the young does not exist in countries that either have a different approach to television or have had little television. In Eastern European countries where television is primarily an instrument for disseminating ideological values, independent observers agree with the official statistics that there has been no significant crime increase amongst the young in countries like Hungary, Poland, or Roumania. And in countries like Western Germany and Holland, where the box is treated far more conscientiously as an informative and educative medium rather than an entertainment one, crimes of violence have actually gone down over the past decade.

If it is argued that the three countries with an advanced television history also have a similar historical, technological, linguistic, and philosophical background that might account for this coincidental rise in violence, then we must set such an argument against the generally accepted causes that experts offer for the escalation in American violence. America, it is claimed, is particularly violent in the 1960s because of the Vietnam war, its liberal gun laws, its frontier history, and its racial confrontations. Yet none of these conditions apply to either Britain or Canada who have no frontier history of violence, strict gun laws, no serious foreign war, and no violent racial conflict. Yet each of these two countries—so different from America in their traditional and philosophical approach to violence—have managed to escalate violence amongst the young in almost the same degree as the United States. Britain, America, and Canada undoubtedly have in common similar systems of entertainment-oriented, violence-saturated television.Until some convincing alternative explanation comes along for this odd coincidence, the suspicion that the fifth environmental factor has been a decisive influence in fostering a frightening increase in violence will need some serious rebuttal.

The statistical case is even more formidable when it is backed by the objective findings of American governmental committees and the research of social scientists. Concluded President Johnson's Commission on Violence, 'The preponderance of available research evidence strongly suggests that violence in TV programmes can and does have adverse effects upon audiences—

particularly child audiences.' The findings have been largely ignored.

Said two American psychologists, Leibert and Baron, whose findings were accepted by the U.S. Surgeon General's Report in 1972, 'It has been shown convincingly that children are exposed to a substantial amount of violent content on TV and that they can remember and learn from such exposure. There is a direct causal link between exposure to TV violence and an observer's subsequent aggressive behaviour.'[7] These findings, too, have produced few changes in the volume of violent TV programmes either in America or Britain.

Finally, in this context, one should note the work done by the social psychologist, Dr Urie Bronfenbrenner, whose book on the comparative behavioural attitudes of American and Russian children, *Two Worlds of Childhood*, has been recognized as one of the most important books on child-rearing written in the last quarter of a century. After an intensive eight-year study of the socializing influences and behaviour patterns of Russian and American children, Bronfenbrenner's surveys found an alarming absence of moral and social responsibility amongst American children as compared to their Russian counterparts. American children were more likely to be cruel, inconsiderate, dishonest, less polite, less kind, helpful or orderly, more selfish, and less conscious of a real sense of responsibility than Soviet children, who develop a concern for others and a feeling of community at an early age.[8]

The causes of this relative anti-social behaviour on the part of American children, Bronfenbrenner attributes fundamentally to the diminishing role of the family as a socializing agent. This condition has been brought about by a number of factors including increasing urbanization and economic and technological changes which tend to decrease opportunities for contact between children and parents.

There are two social elements that fill the void created by the weakening of association with parents and other adults—other children and television. 'The vacuum, moral and emotional, created by this state of affairs is filled—by default—on the one hand by the television screen with its daily message of commercialism and violence, and on the other by the socially isolated age-graded peer group, with its impulsive search for thrills and its limited capacities as a humanizing agent,' writes Bronfenbrenner.[9]

Do Bronfenbrenner's studies have anything to say about the behavioural attitudes of British children? 'It is noteworthy that, of all the countries in which my colleagues and I are working now numbering half a dozen in West and East,' he reports, 'the only one which exceeds the United States in the willingness of children to engage in anti-social behaviour is the nation closest to us in our Anglo-Saxon traditions of individualism. That country is England, the home of the Mods and the Rockers, the Beatles, the Rolling Stones, and our principal competitor in tabloid sensationalism, juvenile delinquency, and violence. The difference between England and America in our results is not great, but it is statistically reliable.'[10]

Dr Bronfenbrenner might also have added that England is also America's principle competitor in the provision of entertainment-oriented, violence-saturated television.

In 1976, when the BBC's charter and the commercial TV companies' contracts come to an end, the nation has an opportunity for changing the goals and direction of its broadcasting services. Judging by the history of television as recorded in these pages, it is not likely that any significant alterations will take place. The argument will be about details—who will get the fourth channel, should the BBC be split up, how will it be financed—rather than any serious recognition of what place television has in our society and how it can be used to further the goals of our society.

Since neither political party has any positive approach to the role that television ought to play as a socializing influence, the easy way out will be taken and the structure of broadcasting more or less left as it is. Every serious investigation of television since the advent of the commercial channel has expressed unease and dissatisfaction with the over-all results of a system that forced the BBC and the ITV to compete with each other for popularity at peak times.

The latest strictures on the system were contained in the Report of the Select Committee on Nationalized Industries which found the Independent Television Authority, since early 1972 re-styled the Independent Broadcasting Authority, 'too much influenced by the needs of the companies which are its agents, too cautious in testing new forms of programmes and in affording greater access to the medium and insufficiently responsive to the public as well as to those working in the industry.'[11]

This Commons Committee also criticized the commercial channel for failing to provide an adequate quota of serious programmes at peak times. It reported that within prime viewing time 'the percentage of serious programmes is less than the stipulated 30 per cent.' It did not state that the actual percentage of serious programmes at peak time was usually between 5 % and 10 % of its total output. Nor did it report on what this level of popular programme did to BBC 1 in an effort to compete for mass audiences.

'The Authority implied that much of the criticism about programme output stemmed from an over-intellectual attitude which was inappropriate for a broadcast service created for the general public,' reads the Report. 'Your Committee felt that these views did little justice to the concern expressed. This was not about the showing of esoteric programmes but about freeing a service to produce its best creative output rather than repeat the safe formulae which previously persuaded a mass audience not to switch off. . . . Your Committee consider justified criticisms voiced that the output at prime viewing times and with it the opportunity to extend the public's range of experience fell below the requirements of the Act.'[12]

While politicians can produce a serious analysis of broadcasting of this kind in which they recognize the need for more responsible broadcasting, greater diversity of output and more serious programmes at peak times, more opportunities for access, participation and dissent on the medium, they behave, as we have seen, quite differently when they are in power. A programme like *Yesterday's Men*, which was an innocuous bantering look at the fate of Labour Ministers in opposition, sent Harold Wilson and his immediate circle into paroxysms of fury. An attempt to produce a full-scale enquiry on Ulster—even when chaired by such a non-explosive trio as Lord Devlin, Lord Caradon, and Sir John Foster, MP—brought the full rage of the Government upon the BBC for daring to air such a sensitive subject in delicate times.

How severe the pressures against independence are upon those who run broadcasting can be judged by the exasperated tone of Lord Hill's remarks in the 1972 BBC Handbook. 'Although we welcome criticism and listen to advice, our programme decisions are our own,' he wrote. 'Anyone who attempts to influence them improperly, whether in or out of Government, will be told to mind his business. . . . There are some who resent our independence, and seek to put us under restraint for their own ends. They are a varied group, and they have different ends—often incompatible ends—but they agree on one thing: that an independent BBC does not suit their book.'

When it is remembered that Lord Hill's appointment as BBC Chairman by Harold Wilson was widely interpreted as an attempt to make the Corporation more amenable to the views of politicians, this declaration on the eve of Hill's retirement shows how essentially incompatible the goals of politicians and broadcasting must always be. Politicians must offer the electorate courses of action and broadcasters must subject those courses of action to the scrutiny of comment and the test of criticism. Inevitably, some politicians will resent either comment or criticism or both.

What Lord Hill had failed to realize was that the Corporation's drift toward popularity by concentrating on the provision of entertainment, had alienated from the BBC those very people who would have defended its right to independence. If the BBC's approach to public-service broadcasting was to be no different from that of its commercial rivals, why should it receive the entire revenue from license fees? Why should it be free of advertising? Why should it be in control of the major share of the nation's broadcasting—two TV channels and national radio —and not be accorded the same limited duties and responsibilities as its lesser broadcasting rivals?

It is obvious that before 1976 a full-ranging enquiry into broadcasting must be undertaken. The Commons Select Committee recognized this need. But such an enquiry must not only concern itself with a tinkering with the present structure, a cosmetic job that will leave the broad philosophical basis of television's function much where it now is. If the entertainment bias of television can produce social effects such as we have seen through its heavy dosage of action/adventure shows and the BBC's over-indulgence in sports programmes, the need for a change of direction would be manifest without enquiring into what other baleful influences it is having on society, and particularly the young.

It is obvious that if there is to be more participation and access to the medium that more television hours and facilities will be needed. This would mean not merely a fourth channel, but also more hours on the available channels to enable the wide range of British life—its arts, its sciences, its industries, its trade unions, its universities, its farms—to get some representation on the box. None of this can be done while entertainment programmes dominate most of the important time-segments and actors, comics, singers, quiz-masters are considered the main inheritors of the medium.

Whatever the terms under which television operates, they must apply to all channels together. Allowing popular channels to compete against specialist or cultural ones will merely mean the bulk of viewers will be subjected to all the dubious influences that an entertainment-biased system produces and will also further fragment society between those who get their views from a frivolous sector of the box and those who acquire them from a more socially committed and demanding sector.

A starting point towards reversing the accelerating trend towards irresponsible and trivial television would be a binding directive that during peak times all channels must provide at least 33% serious programming. If it is argued that the commercial companies could not operate profitably under such conditions then franchises should be offered to companies that would accept such a condition. If no such private companies turn up—a most unlikely eventuality since a comfortable return on capital could always be earned in such conditions—then the Government should consider how television might be run under the umbrella of a large nationalized Corporation—similar to the way it was run before 1956—and financed through a combination of advertising revenue, license fees and, if necessary, direct Government subsidy. To claim that this would in some way restrict the freedom of broadcasting is, of course, sheer nonsense. Reithian broadcasting was just as free from Government restraint and pressure as broadcasting after it. Nothing in the history of Independent television has revealed that it is more zealous and active in resisting outside pressure than the BBC with its non-profit-making structure. On the contrary. It has been the Corporation that has from time to time been in the forefront of fights for independence, while the commercial companies, with rare exceptions, have concentrated on keeping out of trouble. Countries like Sweden, West Germany, and Holland have also managed to produce public-service and popular television— free of Government interference—financed either by a license fee alone or by a combination of license fees and advertising revenue.

Until now the underlying trouble with the structure of British broadcasting has been caused by more concern about how it should be financed than by what it should be doing. If the need for advertising revenue demands the conversion of the medium into a dubious and dangerous national toy then it is obvious that advertising revenue must play second place to the national good. When the BBC was a monopoly, it was clear that it had to serve the national interest and its own interest at the same time. At present its priorities seem to be, first, its own survival by justifying its popularity with the public and, second, the national interest.

Since the BBC and the commercial companies are now more intent on winning the ratings game than concerning themselves with the effects that their competitive posture for popularity is having on the mental and social health of the nation, some body such as a Broadcasting Council is needed to supervise their activities in view of the national good. Free of Government control and influence, it could lay down the necessary rules for providing a broadcasting service that lifted the levels of social debate and intercourse rather than lowered them. Its function would be to guarantee that the competitive ego clashes between rival channels did not diminish the socializing and creative responsibilities of the medium. Its prime duty would be to ensure that the most powerful medium of our time conscientiously reflected the true values, the cultural heritage, and the life style of the nation.

NOTES

CHAPTER I

1. William A. Belson, *The Impact of Television* (London, 1967) pp. 212 ff.
2. Marshall McLuhan, *The Gutenberg Galaxy* (London, 1962) p. 130.
3. Quoted by Asa Briggs, *History of Broadcasting in the United Kingdom*, Vol. II (London, 1965) p. 414.
4. Denis Forman, *The Listener*, 7 December 1967, p. 738.
5. Briggs, op. cit., Vol. I, p. 365.
6. Harman Grisewood, *One Thing at a Time* (London, 1968).
7. H. H. Wilson, *Pressure Group* (London, 1961) p. 81.
8. Ibid., p. 100.
9. W. Altman, D. Thomas, and D. Sawers, 'TV from Monopoly to Competition and Back?' (Institute of Economic Affairs, Hobart Paper 15, 1962).
10. *Hansard*, 23 June 1952, Vol. 502.
11. H. H. Wilson, op. cit., p. 125.
12. Ibid., p. 214.
13. The early finances of the commercial companies are discussed in Burton Paulu, *British Broadcasting in Transition* (London, 1961).
14. *Report of the Committee on Broadcasting 1960*—The Pilkington Report. (H.M.S.O., 27 June 1962) p. 14.
15. E. G. Wedell, *Broadcasting and Public Policy* (London, 1968) p. 118.

CHAPTER II

1. Anthony Howard and Richard West, *The Making of the Prime Minister* (London, 1965) p. 227.
2. Ibid., pp. 222–23.
3. *The Guardian*, 13 August 1968.
4. *Daily Mail*, 21 July 1965.
5. *The Guardian*, 4 October 1965.
6. *The Sunday Times*, 31 October 1965.
7. Lord Simon of Wythenshawe, *The BBC from Within* (London, 1953) p. 51.
8. Op. cit., p. 121.
9. Reginald Bevins, *The Greasy Pole* (London, 1965) p. 116.
10. Op. cit., p. 122.
11. Ibid., p. 123.
12. *The Spectator*, 1 September 1967.
13. *The Sunday Times*, 9 March 1969.
14. *The Times*, 10 February 1968.
15. Ibid.
16. Op. cit.
17. *The Sunday Times*, 30 July 1967.
18. *The Observer*, 30 July 1967.
19. Quoted in the autobiography of Lord Hill of Luton, *Both Sides of the Hill* (London, 1964) pp. 119–20.

20. Ibid., pp. 233–35.
21. The first Chairman of the ITA was the art historian Sir Kenneth Clark (1954–57). The second was the diplomat Sir Ivone Kirkpatrick (1957–1962).
22. *The Times* Parliamentary Report, 10 July 1963.
23. Ibid.
24. *Hansard*, 10 July 1963.
25. The three companies whose financial structure was changed in this way were Rediffusion, TWW of Wales, and Scottish TV. TWW was the only company to completely disappear. The other two maintained their financial interests under a new arrangement.
26. *The Times*, 25 July 1968.
27. For an account of Reith's relations with BBC Chairmen and Governors, see A. Briggs, op. cit., Vol. II, pp. 413–39.
28. *The Observer*, 3 September 1967.
29. Op. cit., pp. 122–23.

CHAPTER III
1. ATV and Associated Rediffusion started to transmit in September 1955; ABC and Granada began a year later. Some of the regional companies like Border and Westward did not start until 1961.
2. *Daily Mirror*, 11 May 1967.
3. *The Sunday Times*, 3 August 1969.
4. *The Guardian*, 17 April 1967.
5. *The Guardian*, 4 May 1967.
6. *The Economist*, 3 June 1967.
7. These included the *Yorkshire Post*, the *Huddersfield Examiner*, the *Halifax Courier*, the *Scarborough Evening News*, certain Yorkshire co-operative societies and trade unions, Baird TV, and Star Associated Holdings, a Yorkshire-based cinema group.
8. An admirable compilation of newspaper reactions to the entire franchise affair is contained in the Panther paperback, *TV File* by David McKie (London, 1968).
9. *The Times*, 30 June 1967.
10. JICTAR stands for the Joint Industry Committee for Television and Advertising Research. TAM—replaced by JICTAR—were the initials of Television Audience Measurement.
11. Interview with James Thomas, *Daily Express*, 24 July 1969.
12. *The Sunday Times*, 2 August 1969.
13. *The Sunday Times*, 3 August 1970.
14. *Television Today*, 10 July 1969.
15. *The Times*, 8 August 1969.
16. *Daily Express*, 24 July 1969.
17. *The Sunday Times*, 3 August 1969.
18. *Daily Mail*, 11 September 1969.
19. They were Humphrey Burton, head of drama, arts, and music; Frank Muir, head of entertainment; Derek Granger, head of plays; Terry Hughes, executive producer of feature programmes; Doreen Stephens, head of children's programmes, religion, and adult education; Joy Whitby, executive producer of children's programmes.
20. *Daily Mail*, 20 September 1969.
21. *Evening Standard*, 19 September 1969.
22. *Campaign*, 3 October 1969.
23. *Financial Times*, 11 September 1969.

24. Ibid.
25. *The Times*, 6 January 1970.
26. *Daily Mail*, 9 January 1970.
27. Under a new arrangement, Post Office affairs were now the responsibility of a nationalized board. The newly named Minister had the same responsibilities over broadcasting as his predecessor.
28. *Television Today*, 23 April 1970.
29. *Evening News*, 21 April 1970.
30. Other men named in the original prospectus, such as Cyril Bennett and Humphrey Burton, also drifted back to the company in an executive or programme capacity.

CHAPTER IV
1. *New Statesman*, 3 October 1969.
2. Hugh Greene, *The Third Floor Front* (London, 1969) pp. 13–14.
3. *The Sunday Times*, 23 March 1969.
4. Op. cit., pp. 58–9.
5. Ibid., p. 63.
6. *Pilkington Report*, p. 213.
7. Ibid., p. 230.
8. Ibid., p. 211.
9. Ibid.
10. Ibid., pp. 42–6.
11. Ibid., pp. 51–68.
12. Greene, op. cit., p. 62.
13. Bevins, op. cit., p. 86.
14. *Evening Standard*, 3 December 1964.
15. *The Sunday Times*, 16 March 1969.
16. Ibid.
17. T. C. Worsley, *Television: The Ephemeral Art* (London, 1970) p. 77.
18. *Evening Standard*, 3 December 1964.
19. BBC Handbook 1966, p. 13.
20. Mary Whitehouse, *Cleaning Up TV* (London, 1967) p. 23.
21. Greene, op. cit., pp. 135–36.
22. *Evening Standard*, 10 March 1964.
23. Joan Bakewell and Nicholas Garnham, *The New Priesthood* (London, 1970) p. 236.

CHAPTER V
1. G. M. Trevelyan, *English Social History* (London, 1942) p. 281.
2. Pierre Daninos, *Major Thompson Lives in France* (London, 1955) p. 148.
3. The Rev. Gordon E. Moody, *The Facts About the Money Factories* (London, 1972) pp. 9–12.
4. Ibid., p. 45.

CHAPTER VI
1. *The Sunday Times*, 9 March 1969.
2. Ibid.
3. *Daily Mail*, 10 May 1969.
4. *The Guardian*, 5 April 1969.
5. Ian Trethowan, *Ariel*, BBC staff magazine, December 1969.
6. *The Observer*, 3 May 1970.
7. *The Sun*, 12 December 1970.
8. Greene, op. cit., p. 59.

9. Quoted in Bakewell and Garnham, op. cit., p. 209.
10. Ibid., pp. 215–16.
11. Greene, op. cit., p. 95.
12. Ibid., p. 101.
13. *The Guardian*, 3 December 1969.
14. *The Times*, 24 March 1971.
15. Quoted in Bakewell and Garnham, op. cit., p. 210.

CHAPTER VII
1. *Newsweek*, 20 March 1972.
2. *Punch*, 20 July 1966.
3. *New Statesman*, 21 June 1968.
4. Milton Shulman, *The Ravenous Eye* (London, 1973).
5. *Violence on Television*, BBC Research Department (London, 1972) p. 7.
6. Ramsey Clark, *Crime in America* (London, 1971) p. 43.
7. *Newsweek*, January 1972.
8. Urie Bronfenbrenner, *Two Worlds of Childhood* (London, 1971).
9. Ibid., p. 116.
10. Ibid., p. 116.
11. *Second Report of Select Committee on Nationalized Industries, Independent Broadcasting Authority* (H.M.S.O., London, 1972) p. lxix.
12. Ibid., p. xxxiii.

INDEX

Index

175

panies, 23, 63, 65, 74, 75, 79; 1964 levy 19–20; Roy Jenkins' Budget, 20, 65, 65*n*; Government relief, 73–5, 79; franchise scandal, 49–50, 55–80 *passim*, 140

Cook, Peter, 92
Cooper, Giles, 140
Coronation Street, 99, 101, 156
Cosmo, 135
Crane, 18
Crawley, Aidan, 58, 67, 72
Critchley, Julian, 69
Crosby, Bing, 21
Crossman, Richard, 113
Curran, Charles, 28, 31, 32, 78, 103, 129, 130, 139, 142

Daninos, Pierre, 109
Day, Robin, 38
Day Lewis, Cecil, 132
Decision, 26; and Harold Wilson, 26–33
De Jongh, Nicholas, 129
Devlin, Lord, 164
Dick Van Dyke, 94
Double Your Money, 18, 64
Dr Finlay's Casebook, 94
Dr Who, 94, 128
Douglas-Home, Sir Alec, 33, 52, 95, 96

Eastaugh, Kenneth, 136
Edelman, Maurice, 36
Eden, Sir Anthony, 11, 97
The Eleventh Hour, 97, 125, 126
entertainment-oriented television, 9, 18–19, 22, 64–5, 72, 76, 81, 87–9, 94, 109, 123, 130, 137–8, 145, 146–67 *passim;* – and violence, 151–6, 159–63; *see also* TV mix, sports on television, ratings
Evans, Geraint, 58, 69

Fairlie, Henry, 27, 28, 31
Federal Communications Commission, 8–9

fforde, Sir Arthur, 42
films (old), TV as vehicle for, 18, 105–6, 123
Forman, Denis, 10
Forster, E. M., 132
The Forsyte Saga, 92, 128, 144
Fortune, John, 97
fourteen-day rule, 10
fourth Channel, 55–6, 79–80
Fox, Paul, 104, 106–7, 110, 123, 137
France, television in, 7
franchise scandal, 49–50, 55–80 *passim*
'The Franchise Trail,' 55
Francis-Williams, Lord, 48
Franklin, Olga, 128
Franks, Lord, 132
Fraser, Sir Robert, 70, 71, 76–7
Free Communications Group, 66, 78, 135
Freeman, John, 56, 58, 72, 79
Frost, David, 56, 58, 67, 72, 96

Gaitskell, Hugh, 11, 27
Gallery, 26, 94, 97
Galsworthy, John, 92
Galton and Simpson, 140
gambling and television, 108, 116–22
Garnett, Alf, 99, 100, 127
Garnett, Tony, 98, 140
General Election, and World Cup, 111–13
General Strike of 1926, 11, 12, 15, 25
Germany, West, television in, 144, 148, 161, 166
Gibson-West, David, 37
Gielgud, Sir John, 132
Gold, Jack, 140
Goodman, Lord, 56
Gordon Walker, Patrick, 15
Government pressure on television, 7, 8, 9, 39, 40, 42, 46, 51–3, 97, 98, 119–22, 147, 166; BBC, 95–6, 103, 145, 164–5; Reith 10–11, 12; ITV 34–6
Grade, Sir Lew, 20, 65, 66, 74, 78